"The beauty of this book is that you can ᴄ ᵍ ₐₐₐᵦₗₑ ₗₑₐₐₑᵣₛₕᵢₚ lessons in small chunks. Open any page and you will find a useful piece of information, a thought provoking point, or a practical approach that you can apply in your role as a manager. These also serve as great discussion starters when meeting with a management or supervisory team.

The tips and ideas that Ian has assembled here transcend borders and cultures; they speak to managers across the globe in developed as well as developing economies."

—HUGH RILEY, Secretary General & CEO
Caribbean Tourism Organization

"The talents one must develop to be a 'best boss ever,' so ably laid out by Ian Cook, are also what volunteer community leaders need to make a difference where they live. Over and over I have seen these very skills and approaches demonstrated by the most effective individuals who go through our programs and make a difference in the regions and communities they serve."

— SUSAN HORNE, President & CEO
LEAD VIRGINIA

"Are you the *Best Boss*? You can be. Pick up Ian Cook's latest book and open it to any page. You will find a thoughtful insight or an easy to implement technique on every page. Ian has done the legwork for you. His suggestions are based on solid research and best practices. He helps you translate the most recent research into practical tips and techniques to improve your results as the 'boss.' He provides solutions and sound advice in areas such as how to engage and motivate your employees, effective ways to improve performance, and suggestions for leading teams for better results.

Throughout the book you will find references to management expertise requirements, interlaced with the guidance for how to make it work for you. And when you close the book you realize that Ian's personalized style stays with you. You'll think about the best practices. You'll implement the technique. And you'll be well on your way to being the *Best Boss*."

—ELAINE BIECH, ebb associates inc, author, *The Business of Consulting*, editor, The ASTD Leadership Handbook

"More than searching for what's new in leadership we need to better understand and apply what works. Ian's done a masterful job of providing his practical coaching and leadership development experience in an easily digested format ready for application. This highly readable selection of timeless leadership principles brings us to the heart and skills of how to be the best boss they ever had!"

—JIM CLEMMER, *Practical Leadership* author, speaker, and workshop/retreat leader, The Clemmer Group

# WOULD THEY CALL YOU THEIR

# BEST BOSS EVER?

## Ian Cook

PRACTICAL TIPS AND
INSIGHTS FOR THE
SUCCESSFUL MANAGER

# WOULD THEY CALL YOU THEIR
# BEST BOSS EVER?

## Ian Cook

### PRACTICAL TIPS AND INSIGHTS FOR THE SUCCESSFUL MANAGER

LEADER'S BEACON

# Contents

# Section 2
# Having The Tough Performance-Related Conversations ...57

# Section 3
# Creating a Motivating Work Environment ......................75

# Section 6
# Leading High Performing Teams ...............................155

## Section 10

# Introduction

One of my favorite ways to begin a management development workshop or a speech is to pose three questions to my audience:

1. Think of the best manager you've ever worked for, your *Best Boss Ever*.
2. What did he or she do? What was it about this manager that causes you to select him/her?
3. Now, how were **you** working for this individual? How motivated were you in your job? How hard did you work? How much of your potential did you choose to contribute? And how did you feel about your job and about yourself?

The answers I get back from question #2 will not surprise you. Typically, they describe managers who are positive, confident, comfortable in their own skin, honest, great listeners, motivated by something beyond their own interests, genuinely caring that their staff succeed and grow in their job, while at the same time demanding high performance and results.

But the really interesting insight emerges when people respond to the third question. They suddenly realize that they, as employees, are inspired to operate at their best when they report to an excellent leader. They are more engaged and productive in their work. They willingly contribute what is sometimes called "discretionary effort," above and beyond what is expected.

*Same employee but reporting to a different caliber of manager; you get different results.*

"This is great, Ian," you say, "but how can I be a higher caliber boss? What specifically can I do.?"

In an attempt to provide some answers to this question, I have selected the best of my posts from the first 18 months of my leadership blog, *Build Best Bosses* (http://www.888fulcrum.com/blog/), and clustered them under ten chapter titles. The first seven titles are "business issue" areas we at Fulcrum Associates Inc. have identified where, if the managers excel, "business" outcomes will be positively impacted. The last three titles certainly support this result.

## How to Draw What You Need from this Book

We all like to graze, in one form or another. We grab the TV remote and surf the channels. We approach a buffet with glee, scanning the array of food items, tipping up the lids to peer into the hot entree containers, and then sampling the ones that seem the most interesting and tasty. We pick up our ipod and spin through our playlists to find one that fits our mood. And, of course, we surf the internet in search of web sites that have the information we need.

I intend this book to be a "field" for you to graze in. You don't need to read the pieces in any particular order, or to read them all, for that matter.

What you will find in these pages are short pieces that are quick and easy to read. They have been inspired by my reading and twenty-four years of working with managers as a workshop leader, executive coach, and facilitator. They are written for busy managers who want to increase their effectiveness as a leader and build stronger teams. They include:
- practical tips and techniques to apply
- nuggets from research in managerial and organizational effectiveness
- new ways of looking at excellence as a manager
- best practices from other organizations

## Managing Others is Never Easy

I have such a deep respect for those who take on the role of manager. It is a tough, complex job to perform well. Bringing the best out in employees and getting results through their efforts is no clear cut science. It involves the nebulous and shifting hopes, perceptions, needs, and fears that human beings—both employees and managers—bring to the workplace. And all this drama takes place within organizational cultures that range from high-performing to toxic.

As management expert Tom Peters puts it:

*"If leadership were just about hitting your numbers, about driving the troops to meet their quotas, then leadership would just be a math problem. But leadership is a human mystery."*

Add to this that many of the managers with whom I have had the privilege of working come from a technical background, be it engineering, science, finance, accounting, or IT. When they move into the realm of people management, the training, skills, and disciplined problem solving approach that have been at the very core of their success no longer serve them well. In other words, their very strengths frequently impede their ability to read, understand and respond to employees.

Of course, I am sure you would love to get your hands on a few silver bullets that will guarantee a productive relationship with your employees. I wish it were possible. If I had them, I would be writing a different—and certainly shorter—book and doing it from my villa on the French Riviera.

Instead, the reality managers face is reflected in this quote from David Whyte in *The Heart Aroused*:

*"Much of our work is bent toward keeping chaos at bay, staving off financial disaster, or integrating the differing wave forms of dozens of unpredictable people in a given organization…wave against wave, work is an uncharted sea. Any difficult conversation, any sudden change of career, we feel, may lead to a possible shipwreck."*

While the pieces in this book are not silver bullets, my hope is that they will give you some practical, usable ideas, provoke your thinking about management and leadership, and perhaps even inspire you.

I salute you on your journey toward being an ever better manager, hopefully to the point that many of the employees you lead will look back on their career and say that you were their **best boss ever!**

# Building the Leadership Impact of Managers

The pressure continues unabated to generate greater results using existing resources. The most critical—and usually the largest—resource is people. To some degree employee contributions can be leveraged through improved technology and more efficient workflow processes. Many leading enterprises have pretty well optimized these approaches.

So, forward-thinking employers now see their leadership—at all levels—and the culture it fosters as the best place to leverage their investment in employees for increased output. The emerging evidence is that the most effective leaders consistently generate superior results.

Furthermore, savvy executives understand that high quality leadership, once in place, is not easily matched by the competition, providing an enduring edge of competitiveness and excellence.

Development strategies that produce such effective leaders must not be confined to just management skills but, more fundamentally, must address the very assumptions and habits of thinking that dictate a leader's actions and responses.

# Four Steps to Effective Performance Management

The Institute for Corporate Productivity has four recommendations for putting in place an effective, robust process for managing and recognizing individual performance.

Focusing, as is their wont, on the practices of high performing organizations, their research has found that:

- Less than 20% of organizations in general have managers who are very highly or at least highly skilled in conducting performance reviews.
- Critical to managing individual performance effectively is to have the right set of skills resident in your managers and supervisors.
- High performance enterprises are twice as likely as low performing ones to provide training in these critical skill areas;
  - » Developing goals
  - » Giving and receiving feedback
  - » Conducting a performance review meeting
- High performers address not only **results** (goals, metrics, etc.) but also the **behavior** that generates the results.

Here, taken verbatim, is their four-part recommendation:

1. **Train managers to deliver effective performance management.** This speaks to developing core skills such as clarifying objectives, giving feedback–regularly, and especially in the performance review meeting, and fostering motivation
2. **Differentiate and reward top performers appropriately.** Identify the extraordinary contributors, your superstars, and reward them accordingly. Make the top merit increase in your organization significantly above what the average employee receives.
3. **Address and resolve poor performance.** Go beyond merely culling the bottom 20% and replacing them. Before resorting to that strategy, explore possible factors leading to the poor performance.

Consider development opportunities, test stretch assignments, outstanding conflict issues, and what has been tried (or not tried) in the past.

4. **Encourage continual feedback.** Don't wait until the end of the year to tell an employee how he or she is doing. Low performers, in particular, need course corrections sooner so they have time to turn things around. High performers also benefit from ongoing feedback. The on-going recognition of work well done will keep your people engaged and on track.

These are so sensible. They offer a straight-forward roadmap to follow. If you are a senior leader, demand, engage in and support a process that does all four really well. Our training program, *The Skillful Leader*, can deliver on items 1, 3 & 4. Your HR folks can, again with your support, devise a system to see that #2 is installed.

All your employees—most importantly your star performers—will appreciate this and your organization will surely reap the greater benefits of everybody contributing more.

# Ouch! It Hurts To Think This Much! (Identifying Performance Targets)

Are your employees clear about what you expect from their performance this year? I should be able to come in as a consultant, sit down one-on-one with any individual who reports to you and ask him or her, "What will constitute 'fully satisfactory' and 'outstanding' performance by you over the current year? Please describe it for me." When I then meet with you and ask the same question about the individual, your answer and theirs should pretty well match.

In working with organizations large and small, I am repeatedly amazed at how few people really know what their priorities are and what performance standards their boss expects them to meet. As a result they assume certain standards or, more typically, they just keep working from day to day until at year-end they receive a surprise "thumbs up" or "thumbs down" in their performance review.

But why don't more managers worldwide do this well? Why don't they identify what they expect from their direct reports? Why do they leave such a vital item as expected results so fuzzy? I mean, WHAT COULD BE MORE IMPORTANT? Let me suggest a couple of reasons. See if these apply to you.

Sometimes the manager truly does not know. Maybe he (or 'she' with this pronoun) has not received clear priorities and expected deliverables for his unit from his own boss. If this is true for you, then obviously you need to have that conversation with your boss about his expectations.

Often, the manager is unable to find the time to articulate performance expectations for each employee. Hey, managers are super busy today. They have more people reporting to them than ever before and they face immediate pressures, fires to fight, sixty-five e-mails to answer and just generally "doing more with less."

But there is a number one reason they don't communicate expectations. Let's face it, it is hard mental work for any of us to decide what we truly want from our employees. We have to think of the various areas of each person's job and determine what level of output is fair to expect and what standards we will measure it against. Besides, frequently we don't know that much about a particular job. We may never have performed it ourselves.

Here is my advice. Take the time! Map it out. Have your employees themselves identify key result areas for their job and suggest the numerical indicators or observable behaviors to be reviewed during the year and at review time. This will enable your people to plan their activity, commit to results and self-monitor their progress towards goal achievement.

Communicating performance targets is not some extra task that keeps you from "the real work." It is at the very core of being a *professional leader/manager*.

# Time to Check for Blinders, Manager

I recently read an article by Ezra Klein that made a strong case for **not** raising the age of eligibility for social security. In the U.S. it is going from 65 to 67.

I have always assumed–without a lot of thought, I might add–that raising the retirement age was a no brainer way to reduce the funding strain on government, especially to cover us baby boomers now massively arriving at our golden age. Hey, we are living much longer. Why not extend the period of years that we have to be gainfully employed.

The article brought to my attention, however, that most jobs people do require them to stand for long periods, do physical work, and, by the way, some are just really mind-numbing. They will not be as ready as I, a knowledge worker, to embrace the idea of working longer than their parents did.

Now, I don't want to get into the content of the issue of keeping Social Security solvent or of the social justice merits of making blue collar workers toil longer.

What I do want to raise here was **how absolutely oblivious I have been** to potential serious consequences to manual laborers of having to work a few more years. I like to work. I don't intend to stop doing my training presentations, facilitating, and coaching until I'm into my 70's. It's interesting work and not too strenuous as long as I exercise regularly, eat and sleep well.

I just assumed that what works for me should be applied to everyone. And tell those who disagree with me to "get over it." I have been a captive of my perspective!

The view from the manager's perch is different than from the employee's. And an important, ongoing challenge for managers is not to become captive to that perspective.

# Leading and Managing: Are They Really So Different

I'm deep in the middle of Henry Mintzberg's new book, *Managing*. While not a light read, he does take his typically provocative stand:

"Instead of distinguishing managers from leaders, we should be seeing managers as leaders and leadership as management practiced well."

While we may be able to separate the two forms *conceptually*, asserts Mintzberg, you can't disentangle the two *in practice*. This has a certain resonance with me. It has always felt a tad artificial to separate leading and managing, although our programs have positioned the former as more influencing and big picture thinking, vs. the skill-based nature of pure managing.

So, how do *leading and managing* intermingle as the "manager" goes about her duties? Mintzberg has a practical model of what the manager does. She works her magic by operating on **three planes**, each of which involves both an internal (i.e. within the unit) and external focus.

1. **Information** – Collecting, organizing, authoring and communicating information out into the wider organization and beyond as well as down into her own unit. She uses information to suggest, cajole, and frame certain actions and decisions on the part of unit employees and others outside the unit.

2. **People** – Encouraging, helping and developing (i.e. leading) individuals and teams within her unit to make decisions, get things done and develop new capacities to perform. On the "people plane" you also have linking to people outside the unit, for example, building relationships with individuals in other departments, customers, vendors, public officials, and so on. Here is where a manager's networking skill is so critical.

3. **Action** – Internally, it means getting directly involved, hands-on, in key decisions, projects and problems. Beyond the unit, the manager makes deals to mobilize support for the unit's needs and interests by exchanging reciprocal power and influence.

When you think about it, working these three planes internally and externally, the manager has to slide back and forth, frequently during the same interaction, from leading to managing. At one moment she is directing her staff to move on certain priority tasks. Then she represents her department at a senior team meeting. Then she negotiates with finance for leniency on reporting requirements just this month. Then she meets with an irate customer company, listening and problem-solving their complaint.

In the end, says Mintzberg, managing is a "soft" craft (with an element of art thrown in), not a hard science. This is why management training and leadership development can be a difficult "sell" to technically-oriented decision makers. Craft though managing may be, the strategic importance of developing the leadership roles of your managers is in no way diminished.

# The Manager's Most Important 3 Feet

A professional speaker colleague of mine, Sam Geist, talks about the most important three feet for a sales person—that three foot distance lying between you and your customer. He even hands out yardsticks at his keynote presentations to burnish this point in the minds of his audience.

In a similar vein, I put it to you that your most important three feet **as a manager** is that space between you and your employee. I'm not talking about so much about the physical space but more importantly about the mental and emotional space. How you handle this "I-thou" space will determine how effective a leader you are. It's a distance across which pass—in both directions—information, meaning, expectations, resistance, appreciation, criticism, enthusiasm, hope, discouragement, fear, and much, much more.

We hear a lot these days about employee engagement, productivity, and retention, about talent development, and about leadership. These are all central to the results your employees ultimately generate and how profitable and successful your enterprise will be in creating wealth and achieving its goals.

Look at the organizations that do these things well and trace back to what's behind it. Your search will eventually take you to that same "yardstick" of distance across which exemplary managers are leading excellent relationships with their employees. This is where the important work of leaders at all levels lies.

# Great Management Tips for Uncertain Times

Scads have been written about how to lead your people, keep them motivated, and mitigate the stress-and-worry effects of the recession. Here's a really comprehensive article from *Workforce Management*, entitled, "Managing During the Downturn" (http://www.workforce.com/archive/feature/hr-management/managing-during-downturn/index.php).

The authors do a great job of providing managers with practical strategies to deal with four realities of work life in tough times:

1. Fear of becoming unemployed
2. Emergence of "us vs. them" behavior in your company
3. Pervasive, ongoing, unfocused anxiety
4. High stress that can turn into distress

This lengthy article is worth your time to read in its entirety. As the authors point out, your organization is not a counseling clinic. Nevertheless, they offer some solid, doable ideas that you can implement to help your employees cope with the psychological impact of this cursed recent economy from which we are all slowly pulling ourselves free.

# Why Managers (Too Often) Solve it Themselves

How often do you jump in and solve your employees' problems for them? Probably more often than you would like and, if you are like most other bosses, more frequently than you should. Whether your employee brings you a problem/question or you are addressing a performance shortfall on his or her part, it is really, really tempting just to give him/her the answer and get on with life.

Here are four reasons that explain managers' tendency to default to a directive style. See if you can relate to any of these in yourself and perhaps in other managers where you work.

1. **Managers have previously developed the "take action" habit.** Most of them are promoted from the ranks of individual contributors where they worked in a technical, professional, administrative or blue collar activity. Here success came from organizing and controlling inanimate "things," such as reports, data, concepts, materials, and so forth. Their job was to take some kind of action or make some decisions around these items. They come to management having already developed a "default," action-oriented response to their work.

2. **A manager's key success factor is his or her ability to identify and solve problems.** Managers are constantly being presented with urgent issues. When they solve one they feel good. They feel like they have added value to the operation. So, it's not surprising that when an employee brings forward a problem the manager's default response is either to solve it himself/herself or tell the employee how to solve it.

3. **They most likely already know the solution.** Managers typically have been around longer than many of their employees and have learned a lot about working effectively. Furthermore, if they came up from the ranks, they understand the front line work from personal experience. Often the solution is a no brainer to them. Without duct tape to cover their mouth, it is hard to keep themselves from blurting out the answer.

4. **Managers are busy people.** It is simply quicker to give the answer, check it off mentally as another problem solved, and send the employee on his/her way. Any other response, such as coaching the staffer to come up with a good solution, will take more of the manager's limited time.

If you can see one or more of these forces operating within you, you have reached the first step toward changing your default behavior to one of coaching and getting your employees do the mental heavy lifting around problems they encounter in their work.

# You Gotta Get'em to Wanna:
# 6 Roles the Modern Leader Plays

So much is changing in our economic and business environment these years, is it any wonder that the nature of leadership is changing too? We're not talking a new fad, here, folks. Fads come and they go. Leadership—as it is progressively practiced today—is here to stay! If you manage, supervise, direct or formally influence other people, you lead them! So, just for the record, what does this new style of leadership comprise?

I have always liked this distinction: "management" is getting things done through others; "leadership" is getting others to want to get things done. Howard Gardner, chronicling some great 20th century leaders in his fascinating book, *Leading Minds*, calls a leader "an individual who, by words and/or personal example, significantly influences the thoughts, feelings, and/or behaviors of... human beings." Leadership now is really the practice of influencing.

But why is influencing becoming the preferred way? What is wrong with just telling them, from your own experience and authority base, what to do? Allow me to offer two good reasons.

First of all, the processes to provide most products and services have become complex. No one person alone has the answer any more. People are increasingly called upon to communicate and make decisions laterally with others, rather than vertically through the boss. In my own consulting practice I am seeing more cross-functional teams, greater sharing of vital information, and more involvement in the ranks. I am frequently being asked to assist in initiatives to break down walls between those darn "silos."

Secondly, today's more complex work demands high levels of skill and knowledge. Employees, the so-called "knowledge workers," who possess these assets are in great demand. They seek the challenge of contributing their ideas and using their heads in their work. This is what they are being paid for. These people do not tend to hang around when you become overly directive with them.

So, what is a well-meaning manager or supervisor supposed to do? How does he or she operate as a leader in today's emerging high performance organizations? My advice is to concentrate on six roles that, together, earn you the right to call yourself a "modern leader."

1. **Servant Leader**

   Robert Greenleaf coined the term. The idea is that the best leaders see themselves as servants first. Decide whom—not what—you serve in your leadership capacity. Help them succeed in contributing to the organization, help them learn and grow, and see them as your "customer" (for your leadership services).

2. **Direction Setter**

   Communicate the overall goals of the company so that they are understood. Engage your people in crafting individual and team objectives that support these wider goals. If you are a unit leader, your job is to ensure that the energy and priorities of your group are aligned with the organization's strategic direction.

3. **Steward for high standards and results**

   No matter how much you share decision-making power and involve your people, you are still ultimately responsible for the results being achieved and the objectives being met. Insist on high standards, for yourself, of course, and for those you lead. This means dealing with those who choose to underperform. As W. Somerset Maugham once said, "It's a funny thing about life. If you refuse to accept anything but the best, you very often get it."

4. **Motivator/Coach**

   Yes, you do have a role in—but by no means 100% responsibility for—motivating your people. That direction you articulated in (2) above…add your passion about it. Enthusiasm is contagious. It is also motivating. Help them identify what they truly desire (the WIIFM, if you are in sales) from their work and career. Do what you can to help them achieve this.

5. **Changemaster**

   You will never stop being called upon to lead, or at least support, change initiatives. All humans, are forced on a psychological journey when faced with change. The journey takes one from "endings" through a "neutral zone" and finally into a period of "new beginnings." William Bridges' excellent book, Managing Transitions, lays out clearly how to manage people at each of these critical stages

6. **Role Model**

   Leadership manifests itself, above all, in how you behave. On what to you focus your attention? your time? your questions? Do you act consistently with your values? For example, if you espouse an open, trusting work culture, do your people find it "safe" to speak their mind to you?

Make no mistake about it! These six roles are at the core of leadership in the coming years. Give them a central place in your set of attitudes and skills and you will be better, do better and feel a whole lot better as you serve others…from out in front.

# "It's About the Caring, Stupid!"

Political consultant James Carville provided the now famous (in the US, at least) phrase format for directing laser-like attention to the issue that presents the highest leverage. Leadership blogger Steve Roesler, in a posting on his blog, *All Things Workplace*, reminds us what the Towers Perrin and other surveys have uncovered. In Steve's words,

> *"Employees relate their success on the job to feeling cared for and about. Not money, not flex time, but feeling that people above them (emphasis added) care about their well-being."*

Too many managers, under constant pressure to deliver results, forget that people are people, not machines. The vast majority of solutions organizations put in place to motivate staff are in the form of carrots (give them some stuff) and sticks (scare them with consequences–fear–should they choose not to perform well). Now of course, the former are appropriate, as part of the value proposition to employees. The latter are also appropriate, **following** a pattern of poor performance.

But what really turns the motivational crank of most humans who also happen to be your employees is the belief that their boss and, especially, senior management genuinely care about them as *people*, as opposed to just strategic human resource assets.

This means that, as a leader, you need to be in touch with how much you–truthfully, now–**care** about those who toil for the enterprise and, in particular but not exclusively, report to you. This requires some soul searching on your part. Do you really care or are you just pretending to, perhaps fooling yourself that you do?

If you come to the realization that you have, in fact, been pretending, I have news for you. They already know.

# Talent Magnets

In my leadership workshops and keynote speeches I sometimes ask the group/audience to think of the best boss and worse boss they've ever had, what each did, and what effect it had on you.

People come up with all kinds of descriptors and behaviors of both bosses. But one thing emerges about the *best boss ever* (BBE). **He/she is someone you want to work for…and keep working for.**

Furthermore, a BBE is almost always someone for whom others would like to work for too. When an internal posting for a position in his/her department opens up, many people apply. They know that he/she will inspire them, give them opportunities to do their best work, encourage them, challenge them, and develop them. And that BBE doesn't take himself/herself too seriously; there's a refreshing humility emanating here.

BBE's are "talent magnets." I really like that term. I love the visual image of their drawing excellence to them and then of the synergy that results when all that talent starts working together.

But these "best bosses ever" don't just aggregate talented employees. They nurture and grow the capacity and potential of their people. And, more than is the case with average managers, their people move on and up in the organization to new and greater contributions to the enterprise's success. In other words, with the most talented employees, a form of reverse polarity at some point takes place.

Alas, methinks I stretch the magnet metaphor a bit too far.

# Qualities of The Top CEO's

**Robert Rosen**, CEO of the management consulting firm Healthy Companies International, reported in the July/2010 issue of *Leadership Excellence* magazine on conclusions gleaned from interviews of top executives in forty countries over the past 20 years. He and his team was looking for the attributes of the best leaders.

They singled out five key characteristics:

1. **Genuine.** They naturally connect with and engage people. They are open and transparent about themselves and about hearing what others think. They foster trust through their authenticity.

2. **Comfortable with uncertainty.** Fully aware and unworried by the truism that the past does not predict the future, they maintain a healthy distance from the status quo and remain open to what changing conditions bring to their enterprise. And they adopt the psychologically healthy strategy of transforming anxiety around uncertainty into productive energy to move forward.

3. **Intensely focused on the human side of the business.** Seeing their people as THE core driver of the company's success, they invest in, develop, effectively deploy, and nurture their workforce.

4. **Committed to growth.** It is the focus of their attention and their energy. They talk about growth constantly and push their managers to think about it and always operate with it in mind.

5. **Obsessed with execution.** The classic expression, "a bias for action," would not be strong enough here. These executives are always taking action and insist that their employees do too.

This is obviously not the only or even the definitive list of top leader attributes. It is a good reminder, however, of what you should be including in your style if you sit at or even near the top of your organization.

# We'll Never Really "Solve" Organizational Life

In his newly revised book on change, *Beyond the Wall of Resistance*, my colleague Rick Maurer includes an interview with author/consultant **Geoffrey Bellman**. Bellman's response contains some wisdom that helps us all understand the truth about thriving in organizations (and, for that matter, in life).

> *"At the base of it all, we're all a bunch of naked human beings. Down underneath it all, in the game we never talk about—the primary game—we're all down there reaching, grasping, clinging, lifting, floating through life.*
>
> *But we seldom acknowledge this. We're all equal in that regard. We all share a resistance to looking into the deeper meaning of what we are doing.*
>
> *Let go of the idea that we are ever going to fully understand it, but always keep trying to understand the unspoken game. We are always going to be discovering more about ourselves, our games. We need to acknowledge that the game goes beyond our ability to make sense of it. It is a fascinating life mystery."*

Then he goes on, now talking as a consultant:

> *"Whenever I tell clients to "Do this," "Don't do that," I imply that the game is "solvable." It is not. My advice, my techniques, tools, and models are only attempts at fuller understanding; these tools will not give me answers, the complete picture."*

This is such a powerful reminder to all of us who coach, whether you are a manager or an independent like me. We can't "fix" things for those we coach. And we owe it to tell those same people—and ourselves—that there is no ultimate solution to the challenges of swimming in a particular organizational soup. There is only the prospect of continuing to become a gradually better swimmer.

# True Leaders Leave a Huge Hole

I was struck by a local news item in *The Washington Post* on Brian Betts, a model middle school principal, who was found gunned down in his home. While the story obviously includes the murder aspect, I was touched by the leadership angle.

**Rising to a challenge:** Here was a white man who took over a school that was struggling, in a lower income community that is predominantly African America and Hispanic. Furthermore, he talked openly with parents and students about it.

**Open to innovative ideas:** He abolished recesses, believing that the time could be better used for instruction. When a group of graduating 8th graders proposed that he create a grade 9 in the school so they could stay under his tutelage for one more year, he listened, invited them to pitch the idea to the DC School Chancellor, and they won both of them over for not only a grade 9 but also a grade 10.

**Resilent:** Undaunted by first year academic test scores that were disappointing, Betts kept working with his staff, encouraging them to come up with ways to raise the results.

**Operating from deeply held beliefs and values:** He did not accept the prevailing wisdom that you can't change academic achievement in the midst of poverty and broken families. Rather, he held himself and his staff responsible for changing the student results.

**Leading by example:** He cooked dinners for his students, tracked their progress, and admonished them when they didn't do their homework. Most mornings would find Betts out in front of the school, literally hugging arriving students, encouraging them along and catching a few moments of conversation with parents who dropped them off.

But most of all, in two short years Brian Betts has **left a legacy**. Here's how we know.

- "Every time he saw me, I was one-third his. I was a little immature. He straightened me out. He kept in my hair about everything when I did something wrong." (Current student)

- "The worse the students were, the more he wanted to teach them. It was all he talked about." (Colleague)
- "I can't explain the kind of impact this guy had on my life." (Former student)
- "He watched out for the children and everything that didn't look right: drugs, guns, violence." (Parent)
- "He will be hard to replace but, in less than two years, he has set a standard for learning at Shaw that will last a long time." (Washington Post education columnist)

Brian Betts reminds us of what leadership looks like at when it rocks. Imagine what it would be like if just a quarter of our leaders were like Brian Betts!

# R-E-S-P-E-C-T

The inaugural issue of The Korn/Ferry Institute's quarterly journal, *Briefings on Talent & Leadership*, has an article on one of the giants in the study of Leadership, Warren Bennis. Apparently Bennis tells his students at the University of Southern California a story about a young U.S. Army officer that was commanding a squad that entered the Shiite holy city of Najaf in 2003.

They found themselves suddenly surrounded by an angry and increasingly volatile mob. Then, at a pivotal moment which could have tipped into civilian blood being shed, the commander did something remarkable:

> *He held his rifle high above his head and pointed the muzzle toward the ground. He ordered his squad to do the same. Then he barked, "Take a knee!" and the soldiers sank to the ground in a nonthreatening posture. Startled by the action, the crowd grew quieter and then started to move away. The officer ordered his soldiers to withdraw and the standoff ended without a shot being fired.*

The commander, interviewed by a journalist later, said that what he did came from a snap decision based on an intuitive reaction to the rapidly developing crisis situation. Nothing in his military training taught him this particular approach as a response. He just read the context of what was happening and acted.

Bennis shares this brief tale as an example of a leader operating out of a core principle of respect, in this case respect for the crowd of Shiite citizens in *their* holy city.

We speakers, trainers and writers in the field of management seldom shine a spotlight on this increasingly critical element of effective leadership. We talk about listening skills, dialogue, and understanding the other point-of-view. But we neglect to mention the importance of **respecting** that other point-of-view! In order To get anything significant done in this crazy quilt of change and confusion in which leaders are operating today, they need to develop the ability to reach out and build bridges, form coalitions, partner with others and seek common ground.

The foundation of those bridges is R-E-S-P-E-C-T.

# Stepping into the Lion's Den

President Barack Obama stands before the Republican House of Representatives caucus and takes direct questions. This is a group that, from the President's perspective, has been opposing his agenda adamantly at every turn. This fascinating event is the closest thing I've ever seen in the U.S. to what people with parliamentary systems know as Question Period (Canada) or Question Time (England).

Leaving aside the political issues and possible motives ascribed to each side for engaging in the event, I think Obama modeled an important element of leadership. This is the willingness to seek out and engage in dialogue those who oppose your ideas or have yet to buy in to your agenda and vision.

Many leaders do this as part of their strategy for implementing change. They hold all-hands staff meetings to explain their vision, share the rationale and benefits of the change, and then respond to questions from the troops. It is even more effective if, at the outset, the leader makes it clear that he/she welcomes expressions of concern and disagreement.

There is tremendous power in putting yourself out there among your fiercest skeptics, listening to and honoring their points-of-view, acknowledging their heartfelt concerns, and then responding with the goal of assuaging their fears and inviting them to see things from your perspective.

# Fear and Managers' Fears

You seldom hear the word "fear" in management development workshops. Of course the word is not welcome anywhere in organizations. It's the "F word" in offices and plants. Odd, isn't it, since fear is always lurking in our workplaces, especially during the last few years of economic hell?

For some inexplicable reason your people think that you aren't worried about your own job or about the brutal labor market you would be thrown into if you lost it. They think only they have fears. But, as you are of course well aware, employees are not the only ones who experience the raw worry that fires up your adrenalin when you wake up at 3:00 AM. Managers too have been feeling the gnawing anxiety of possible cutbacks and downsizing, even if they try valiantly not to show it.

It takes courage not to show your fears to your people. The poet D.H. Lawrence had this to say:

> *"The great virtue in life is real courage that knows how to face facts and live beyond them."*

What you do with your own fears shapes the way you lead. It also influences how worried your staff become because they tend to take their cues from the boss. So, here's the key question: *should you share your own concern, or is it best to pretend that you are fine?* (Or, as they seem to say about everything in Jamaica, "no problem, man.")

I think managers must present a blend to their employees. They should be authentic and admit that there is a risk, a potential downside, based on the current environment. They should even admit that they are concerned about this. But then they should share how they are **choosing** to respond to the situation, things like:

- Working as hard as they can each day to put their department/function and the organization in a position to sustain itself until better times.
- Focusing on what's possible and on solutions, instead of dwelling on what's wrong and on problems.

- Keeping in mind all the things we are doing well and what our strengths are.
- Consciously curbing needless negative and "woe is us" talk.
- Adopting the belief that not only will we survive but we will succeed.

Tell them this is the choice you are making. Invite your people to choose likewise.

# Add Inspiration and Watch Your Leadership Soar

Jack Zenger and Joe Folkman in their book, *The Inspiring Leader*, share a remarkable piece of data about how to move your leadership ability to its full potential. Their research found that far and away the most powerful leadership competency is "inspires and motivates others to high performance."

"So, big deal; no surprise there," you say? Well, here's the neat part. They found that if you have a particular strength in "Inspires Others" and can combine them with two other leadership strengths–"Analytical/Technical Ability" and "Gets Results"–your probability of being what they call an "extraordinary leader" (i.e. rated as more effective a leader than 90% of other managers out there) goes up geometrically. Take a look at what they found the various probabilities to be:

- *Analytical/Technical Ability*, alone – 0.9% (i.e. less than 1%)
- *Gets Results*, alone – 0.8% (again, less than 1%)
- *Inspires Others*, alone – 1.1% (again, just around the same 1%)
- Analytical/Technical Ability & Gets Results, combined – 6.6%

**But, when you have developed a strength in all three competencies your probability of entering the ranks of the 10% most effective leaders rises to an astounding 77%.**

What's the lesson here? While you may be a results-driven leader, you are operating way below your potential unless you develop the ability to tap into the remarkable power of desire and commitment within your team. Inspiration, obviously, is located on the "heart" (as opposed to "head") side of performance.

- What truly excites you about the results for which you are striving? (Other than your own year-end bonus)
- Why should your employees care? What's in it for them? (Hint: "They get to keep their job" is not the right answer.)
- Who will be served if your unit or organization achieves the results? (Beyond your stockholders)

If these questions have not occurred to you thus far in your career, perhaps it's time you started asking them.

# Oh Yeah, Another Thing About Inspiring Leaders

I'm returning to the work of Jack Zenger and Joe Folkman one more time. They found a significant relationship between the degree to which a manager is strong in the leadership competency, "Inspires and Motivated Others," and the percentage of their employees who have thought about quitting.

Only 17% of staff working for the most inspiring & motivating leaders considered quitting, vs. 51% of those who report to the least inspiring managers.

In a blog post (http://zengerfolkman.wordpress.com/2009/11/25/a-monster-of-a-problem-how-to-help-leaders-be-more-inspiring/) Zenger and Folkman lay out this connection and share six ways that you can connect emotionally with the members of the team you lead.

Check it out. It's well worth a read.

# To Flood or Not to Flood—a Test of Leadership

The Premier of Manitoba, Greg Selinger, makes the decision to break the dike near Portage la Prairie and deliberately flood 85 square miles and inundate 150 homes…to prevent an uncontrolled break in the dike that would flood 850 properties occupying 190 square miles along the Assiniboine River. He says it is one of the most difficult decisions he has ever had to make.

The very same day, over a thousand miles to the south, Army Corps of Engineers Major General Michael Walsh calls a similar shot. At his word, a 10-ton floodgate, part of the Morganza spillway lock & levee system, is opened, easing water pressure in the Mississippi River that threatens Baton Rouge and New Orleans. This is a much bigger deluge—covering 3,000 square miles and affecting 30,000 residents, including the towns of Morgan City and Houma.

It reminds me a bit of that dramatic incident in William Styron's novel, *Sophie's Choice*. A sadistic nazi forces a mother arriving at the Auschwitz train depot with her two children to choose one of them to be gassed immediately while the other can proceed with her into the camp.

Sophie's decision is an impossible dilemma because there is not so much as a trace of lesser destruction resulting from one choice vs. the other. Either course of action is equally horrendous and unspeakable. At least with the flood situations there is an optimal choice (of course, not the one that the people being deliberately inundated would choose).

Sophie, Selinger, and Walsh's situations did, however, have a couple of elements in common: the choice has to be made and it has to be made by them. Also, no matter how you choose, real, innocent people will be impacted.

I cringed watching Meryl Streep make her fateful selection in the movie. And no way would I want to have been in Greg Selinger's or Michael Walsh's shoes as they wrestled with their options and arrived at their ultimate decision.

This is the guts of leadership in action. I salute both these men.

# Six Lessons from Public Sector Change Leaders

In July, 2009, Booz Allen Hamilton published an interesting study of leaders in the U.S. Federal Government, entitled "What It Takes to Change Government." (http://www.boozallen.com/consulting/advance-our-government/what-it-takes-to-change-government/what-it-takes-to-change-government-overview) The goal was to determine how key strategies are most effectively led and implemented.

It goes without saying that leaders in the federal sector are encumbered by all sorts of forces, bureaucratic, political and constitutional. Nevertheless, I think the conclusions the researchers reached offer valid lessons for managers in other sectors of the economy.

They studied 11 leaders—at a cabinet or sub-cabinet level—who sought to make significant strategic change in their department or agency, for example, modernizing their structure and processes or transforming to a new agency mission. For comparison, they set up a control group of other government leaders who had generated solid but average accomplishments.

The leaders who were significantly more successful in implementing change...

1.  Used a strategic planning process of some form.
2.  Established performance measures to calibrate progress and ultimate achievement. Furthermore, a key to their success was having only two or three goals, ones that were truly *strategic*, vs. tactical or operational.
3.  Built relationships with external interest groups and with Congress. In other words, they reached out proactively to both external stakeholders and potential opponents.
4.  Collaborated with employees, encouraging their participation. So, they looked internally as well. In addition, they devoted about half of their time actively working internally on the change.
5.  Tied performance appraisal and rewards to achievement of the

strategic goals. This included, in a couple of cases, removing executives who were obstacles to the strategy.

6. Were ready and willing to do a reorganization of their structure, if it was warranted. In fact, three quarters of them did conduct a re-org.

Now, here's the rub. The leaders who were most successful bringing about change were practicing good management behaviors (which includes, of course, the above six) rather than just focusing on classic "change management" approaches.

So, a good change manager is, first-and-foremost, a good people manager. Duh!

# A Nobel Prize for Leadership?

I am once again inspired by *The Washington Post's feature, The Question.* Given all the recent hoo-haw about Barack Obama receiving the Nobel Prize for Peace, the Post asked a panel of experts the following question:

> *If there were a Noble Prize for Leadership, what would the criteria be and whom would you nominate?*

The context of this question, since it involves the Nobel Foundation, is of course global. But the answers of the fifteen panelists reveal some interesting themes that I think apply equally to managers in organizations.

Here are most of the criteria identified and used by the panel members:
- Ideas, communications and actions that improve lives or propel others to release their talent and energy to improve lives in their communities, society, or the world
- Building something important and lasting which no-one else could have done.
- Servant leadership
- Doing things others can't do, taking risks others won't take, and most of all, helping the rest of us journey from one place to another in our view of what is possible and achievable
- Working in the "whitespace" between bureaucratic lines, laboring relentlessly—and often thanklessly—for a greater good
- Acting as role models
- The ability–without the use of force–to change the thoughts, feelings, beliefs, and behaviors of other persons–for the wider good.
- An unquestionable moral authority, committed to doing the right thing and standing for the right principles
- Having demonstrated unusual courage and skill in disappointing their own people at a rate they could absorb, in furtherance of the purpose of resolving a long-standing, seemingly intractable, problem
- Words and actions that inspire people to accomplish great good together

## The Themes

From these I detect three overarching patterns. Every one of these reflects what the research says characterizes our best leaders:

1.  Serving others, something way bigger than yourself and your own aggrandizement.
2.  The courage to push the envelop of what seems possible, taking bold but calculated risks.
3.  Influencing and inspiring others to maximum accomplishment.

## My own response to the question

I would award the "Nobel Prize for Leadership" to someone who has accomplished great things by leading from a more universal outlook and understanding. It would be someone who has pretty much transcended his or her own ego, and who sees humanity as interconnected in a vast system to which we all, ultimately, are contributing.

There aren't too many viable candidates out there. But they certainly include well known people like Mandela and Gandhi…and a host of non-famous individuals in companies, associations and communities across the globe who are quietly leading us to achieve the promise of our individual and collective potential.

How about you, Nobel Award Panelist? What criteria would you apply?

# Leader, You May Be Distracted at the Moment

These are challenging economic times. Executives in organizations and owners of smaller businesses get up each morning with a day of wrestling particularly vicious alligators to look forward to. Let's name a few of the regular reptilian challenges they face: cash flow, retaining customers and clients, avoiding layoffs, coaxing low morale employees to dig down and give that extra effort (that we've been asking for since at least last January). Oh yeah, let's not forget that other ever present alligator with the particularly large teeth–apprehension about losing your own job (or your enterprise, owners out there).

Will you allow me to extend the gator metaphor just a moment longer? Thank you.

We tackle the most menacing alligators that are biting our ankles. Some of them we successfully wrestle to the ground; some keep coming back for another chomp. It's hard, isn't it, to think about anything else beyond these formidable threats when they seem about to devour you.

We are distracted by alligators.

This brings me to a study (July, 2009) by Ipsos Reid Canada indicating that 22% of employees in Canada say their loyalty to their current employer has decreased. That statistic is for the working population in general. In organizations where salaries have been frozen, the number rises to 31% and where staff have actually been cut, it jumps to 36%.

What is happening here? You would think that in a down economy employees would feel more beholden to a company that continues to provide them with full time employment. If anything, they should feel substantial appreciation and loyalty. Ipsos' resident expert on employee engagement, J.B. Aloy, has an explanation: "*Staff who feel their involvement is not acknowledged are more likely to become disloyal.*"

I think Mr. Aloy has it right and that this brings us back to alligators. Staff that remain on the payroll are asked to contribute extra effort despite the uncertainty and despite having to pick up the work of people let go or not replaced. I suspect managers are neglecting to recognize and affirm these contributions not because they don't care or appreciate it. It's just that they have been distracted by those alligators constantly snapping at them.

As frightening and threatening as your immediate problems might be, simply make a point of finding the time to shine some positive light on your staff and their efforts. You have probably retained your best employees. If they are among the group feeling less loyal, expect to lose a number of them as soon as the job market picks up.

Then, rest assured, you will have one giant alligator in your face!

# The Fear Factor

*The Washington Post* in an article posed a leadership related question:

> *Successful leaders are admired, respected and trusted, but isn't the dirty little secret that they also need to be feared?...Is President Obama too much carrot and not enough stick?*

> *A panel of 20 experts in leadership from politics, the military and business were invited to comment. You can read their responses in the context of Obama trying to move Congress around a health care initiative. What the piece brought to mind for me, however, is the typical workplace and that single individual for whom most employees harbor at least some level of fear:* **the boss.**

Is **fear**, in fact, an appropriate option in a manager's range of potential people- management strategies?

I don't think so. Not even when an employee or group is resisting outright. To quote one of the panelists, Yash Gupta, Dean of The John Hopkins Carey Business School, "It's up to the leaders of the organization to communicate these [performance] benchmarks in a clear, constructive, professional way that doesn't imply any kind of threat."

You can certainly be tough. Lay out your expectations and by all means insist on the bar being high. If some of your people fall short of the goals—after a reasonable chance to turn their performance around, do follow through with appropriate consequences.

But instilling fear involves an **upfront threat,** either actual or implied, to punish/hurt the other person, typically by promising to remove any number of items employees value: benefits, raises, promotions, good projects, resources, even continued employment status. The sense of the responses of those on the Washington Post panel is that, while a fear-based approach may generate some limited results in the short term or in a crisis, it will trigger longer term resistance and loss of trust and respect that will haunt the leader who employs it.

Furthermore, panelist **Roger Martin**, Dean of University of Toronto's Rotman School of Management, offered an interesting take on *fear:* "One particular kind of fear is useful for leaders to instill, but only that particular kind. It is the fear of not being part of the leader's campaign. The minute a leader generates a success, followers begin to fear not being part of a successful team and will do whatever they can to avoid that fearful outcome."

This makes sense to me. **The fear here (and that is what it truly is) is conjured up by the employee, not instilled by the boss.** It is how the employee chooses to frame the situation he or she is facing. So, to the extent the manager (1) has a clear vision, (2) comes across as confident about the value and the achievability of that vision, and (3) is trusted and respected by her employees, they will be motivated to get on board with the plan.

Vision, clarity, confidence, trust, respect…hey, don't they sound like the classic elements to strong leadership? And fear just doesn't make the list.

# Something for Male Leaders to Keep in Mind

Jessica Bennett's piece in *Newsweek*, "You Are Your Own Glass Ceiling," (http://www.newsweek.com/2009/08/30/you-are-your-own-glass-ceiling.html) got me thinking. The issue she raises needs to be repeated and kept in the conscious awareness of both men and women.

She talks about the dilemma of women, especially women leaders, who struggle with:

- "Yes,"
- "Be a 'go-getter' but be nice at all times," and with
- "Yes, accomplish but don't brag about it."

While, as Bennett states, girls outnumber boys in academic achievement and graduation and school leadership positions at all levels of the education system, something happens when the mass of these qualified individuals flood into the world of work. Women make up only a quarter of law firm partners and are still famously underrepresented in senior management positions in our medium to large sized organizations.

In her article she quotes from Rachel Simmons' book, *The Curse of the Good Girl*: "…being cautious and apologetic impacts just about every standard measure of success in the workplace: money, accomplishment, recognition." The source of limitations placed on women's success in the work world, of course, extend much wider than just what girls learn are the communication and behavior patterns expected of them.

We talk about there being many ways to lead, from Attila to Ghandi. One thing we men leaders need to realize is that, for women, the window of "acceptable" optional styles is much narrower. They typically walk a fine line between:

1. Expressing their assertive, challenging achievement orientation and being stereotyped as a tough bitch
2. Engaging in supportive, empowering coaching approaches and being seen as too soft

As with all humans confined within the experience of being one gender, I as a male can't really feel what women experience as they–every day–navigate the treacherous waters of these two dichotomies. In the role of a manager, however, we men can certainly acknowledge that women do face these dilemmas and be aware of how we might be contributing to it.

# Assessing Organizational Leaders... Like We Do Political Ones

At a recent leadership conference put on by the Wharton School of Business, one of my favorite historians, Richard Norton Smith, offered 10 ways historians can judge presidents fairly, in the context of their times. The full article about his presentation can be found here: (http://knowledge.wharton.upenn.edu/article.cfm?articleid=2294#) While he talks about American Presidents, I think these apply to political leaders in Canada, Europe and the rest of the industrial democracies.

As I read the piece, I wondered how Norton Smith's ten filters (in bold type, below) would work for assessing those who lead organizations in the private, public and not-for-profit sectors. Let's take a look.

1. **History rewards the risk-takers.** If a leader is to accomplish anything great, she must be willing to step out there on the edge, take a stand, put herself on the line.

2. **A president who actively campaigns for his historical place is engaged in a self-defeating exercise.** Organizational leadership studies highlight the best leaders as those who have transcended the need to make their legacy all about themselves. Instead they treat the welfare of people and the success of the organization as their paramount purpose.

3. **There is no single theory of presidential success.** Today's leaders' triumph or fall short due to a number of variables, some within themselves and some in the "card" (external environment) they have been dealt. So, success may be due to persistence, a tough love corporate turnaround push, building on the work of the prior leader, being the smartest person in the room…or not.

4. **Presidents can only be understood within the context, conventions and limitations of their time.** The style and values of an Andrew Carnegie or Henry Ford may well not work in the age of web 2.0. On the other hand, given the focus and mettle of these gentleman, they would, I am sure, stand out from the crowd even today.

5. **If presidents are governed by any law beyond the Constitution, it is the law of unintended consequences.** This relates to #3, above. A leader who, for example, acceded to her position in the summer of 2008, regardless of what she planned to achieve, was forced to manage the impact of the biggest economic downturn since the great depression.

6. **Presidential power, although awesome on paper, is based largely on moral authority.** Jim Collins (Good to Great), Jack Zenger (The Inspiring Leader), Bob Anderson (The Leadership Circle) and many other thought leaders have chronicled how extraordinary leaders accomplish great things through others and with a strength of character and integrity that enrolls people in the cause. The nameplate on the door just isn't enough.

7. **The president requires a talent for making useful enemies.** If you seek to accomplish anything of substance, if you seek to generate significant change in your enterprise, it's a given that you will stir up resistance and foster "enemies." Instead of giving in, backing down or pulling their punches as a compliant style would dictate, a leader can characterize the opposing position as a rejection of progress and putting the organization's very survival at risk.

8. **Every great president marches to the beat of his own drummer.** Rob Goffee and Gareth Jones, in their book, Why Should Anyone Be Led by You?, talk about the leader managing the tension between (1) revealing/sharing authentically enough of himself for people to get a sense of the human being behind the title but (2) not giving them too much. Leaders should keep some mystery (hence uniqueness) about themselves, what makes them tick, and what they are capable of. I think this then leaves enough onto which followers/staff can project their own desired qualities.

9. **The challenge posed by any crisis is equaled by the opportunity for leaders to forge an emotional bond with the people they lead to gain moral authority and expanded powers.** Richard Norton Smith uses FDR and Lincoln as examples of being able to confront a crisis with bold moves because they had the trust of the people that they would not abuse their power but use it for

the ultimate good of the nation. On a lesser scale, of course, this applies to leaders in organizations. Earning your employees' trust is critical.

10. **Greatness, like beauty, is in the eye of the beholder.** This just underlines the fact that it is followers who make the leader...by seeing her as a leader and then deciding to follow her. Some people do, others don't.

# Judgement More than Expertise

In their wonderful new book, *The Practice of Adaptive Leadership*, Ron Heifetz, Alexander Grashow, and Marty Linsky raise a provocative question that has everything to do with effective leadership at the senior level.

> *"At what level in your organization do people begin to feel and act as if they are valued more for their judgment than for their technical expertise?*
>
> *As people ascend the organization in a managerial capacity, less and less does the value they contribute relate to their technical or functional knowledge. Increasingly, they must apply their judgment and wisdom to issues that are strategic and more complex than they are at the operating level."*

But, being humans, they tend to hold on to and use what has brought them success so far…that good 'ol technical expertise.

How about where you work? Have the executives there let go of the need to for precise, clean, unambiguous solutions to the complex problems they face? Do they keep team meetings focused on operational problems and how to fix them? And do they tend to become quiet and contribute little when the agenda topic is of a bigger picture nature?

And if you are one of those executives, how about you?

# Zappos CEO Models How it's Done

On July 22, 2009 Amazon announced that it was acquiring the popular and progressive shoe company, Zappos. Zappos has been in the limelight over the past couple of years for its open and progressive corporate culture.

On the same day, CEO Tony Hsieh sent out a letter to all Zappos employees. To read it in its entirety: http://blogs.zappos.com/ceoletter.

It struck me how in that letter he modeled their employee sensitive culture. It's not that he deigned to quickly communicate with their workforce. It's what he addressed **at the front end** of the letter! Telling them that he will cover a number of points about the merger, he then said, "First, let me get to the top 3 burning questions that I'm guessing many of you will have."

1. Will I still have a job?
2. Will the Zappos culture change?
3. Are Tony, Alfred or Fred (the top executives) leaving?


What Tony Hsieh did was **start with what was immediately top of mind** for his audience, the employee group. This showed a leader who is tuned in to his employees' feelings–here fears. It also showed a leader who realizes that people won't be ready to focus on other important information until their fears and uncertainty around their own security have been at least somewhat assuaged.

It really comes back to that age-old principle from selling and influencing: the other person is tuned into that famous, most popular radio station, WIIFM (What's in it for me?)

# The Best Leaders: a Paradox

In his epochal book, *Good to Great*, author Jim Collins talked about "Level 5" leaders, the ones who generate the very best results, consistently, over time. Most interesting is that they embody seemingly opposite characteristics. On the one hand, they are modest, humble and self-effacing. Yet in the same person dwells a ferocious resolve to have the organization they lead achieve great results.

Research from *The Leadership Circle* reveals the same dichotomy in the most effective leaders: caring, collaborative, relationship oriented, selfless AND driven toward a vision and decisive around achieving results.

The ability to apparently sustain both sides of the paradox comes with a leader having attained a higher stage of adult development, a more highly developed level of consciousness. They can state clearly what they think and want AND, in the same breath, be open to considering–and even integrating–the ideas, contrary positions and criticisms of others.

But I don't believe these great leaders see this as mastering and balancing opposite tendencies. I don't think they experience the paradox. I think they work and live from a place of integration, above rather than between these seemingly contradictory elements.

Why do I think this? Because of the expanding body of work linking leadership to adult development, as well as a sense of it from a couple of people I've known.

I can't be certain about this, though. I'm not operating from that level…yet.

# The Leader as Authentic Actor

Actors on stage and screen are not genuine. They are fakes. They are playing a part, not themselves. Of course, we expect them to do this and, furthermore, we expect them to do it really well, to convince us that they **are** the character they are playing.

But what about a managers who has to play a part and perhaps not express their fully genuine self in a particular situation? For example,

- In challenging economic times, projecting a confidence he may not fully feel himself
- Being brutally honest with a chronic under performer, with a toughness that she has to stretch to access in herself
- An introverted leader addressing a staff conference using an extraverted enthusiasm that feels phony to him

We want our leaders to be authentic. In fact, **integrity** stands at the apex of any list of qualities of extraordinary leaders. Sometimes, however, the toughest thing a leader is called upon to do is step out of her comfort zone and present a different part of her personality. These are situations when her judgment, experience or intuition tells her it is right, even though it feels anything but natural.

But when this happens, she is not being authentic. What gives? How can we reconcile the paradox?

My answer: give her a pass when she temporarily takes on a different persona, as long as:

1. She has the best of intent for the organization and the individuals involved and
2. She makes this temporary shift in behavior and demeanor in full awareness of her true self, of who (and how) she really is.

# This Leader's Lesson– Culture and Collaboration

In a recent piece in *Newsweek*, Cisco Systems CEO John Chambers was asked, "How are you a different CEO today than you were in 1995, when you first moved into the corner office?"

His answer is worth sharing with you:

> *"When I started, I viewed my job as three main areas: vision and strategy of the company, development and recruitment of the team to implement that vision and strategy, and the need to communicate all of the above.*
>
> *Within about four or five years I realized there was something that many of us do not understand when we take a leadership role: culture. Great companies have very strong and great cultures. A huge part of a leadership role is to drive the culture of the company and to reinforce it.*
>
> *The other thing that has changed dramatically is [a shift] from command and control to collaboration and teamwork. It sounds easy to do, but it's hard, because you are trained that way in M.B.A. school and in law school. Around 80 to 90 percent of the job is how we work together toward common goals, which requires a different skill set."*

Shaping, reinforcing, and modeling a strong, positive, open culture. This is the job not only of the CEO but also, collectively, of the senior leadership team.

Top teams need to include in their strategic discussions (1) what the current culture is, (2) what what they want it to be, and (3) how they are, individually and collectively, drive–or retarding–the organization's transformation to that desired state.

As regards the team/collaboration piece, a manager's capacity must include the willingness to let go of control and involve others. Nothing new or surprising but, for many managers, it's still a tough adjustment to make.

# Choose Stewardship Over Entitlement

Most of us have had the experience, at least once in our career, of working for a boss who loved his/her role because it was all about:

- I'm special (after all, they made me the boss)
- I deserve extra respect (because I'm special, of course)
- I have real power (try opposing me and you'll feel the brunt of it)
- I own this place (let's be clear, this is my operation)
- I'm more important than my staff (not really, but…well, I guess so)

This screams entitlement!, I'm sure you would agree. Power—even the idea of having it—can be intoxicating. It's allure is archetypal; it comes with our wiring as humans. This is why every creature in Middle Earth was trying to nab the ring away of Frodo Baggins and Frodo himself was sorely tempted to succumb to its seduction several times in *The Lord of the Rings*. (So, the archetype extends to hobbits, I guess.)

The problem is that it's hard for the employees of such a manager to feel their hearts go "pitty pat" in response to the cause of the boss's greater glory. We simply won't be as engaged or work as hard as we are capable of working. In effect, such a manager's entitlement mindset runs smack dab into another human archetype: the employee's ever present question, *What's in it for me?* (often referred to as WIIFM)

A manager who aspires to real effectiveness should engage instead in what management consultant Robert Greenleaf called *servant leadership*, in essence, seeing yourself as serving those you manage. Or, to quote Bill George from his terrific book, *True North: Discover Your Authentic Leadership,*

> *"To become authentic leaders, we must discard the myth that leadership means having legions of supporters following our direction as we ascend the pinnacles of power.*
>
> *Only then can we realize that authentic leadership is about empowering others on their journeys.*
>
> *The shift is the transformation from 'I' to 'We.' It is the most important process leaders go through in becoming authentic."*

If ever you feel the tug of that ol' Ring of Power, pause and remind yourself that you are leading a unit or enterprise that has importance beyond your own well being and aggrandizement. You people will sense it. And they will contribute more of their capacity simply because of it.

# Traditionals, Boomers, X, and Y Are People Too

There is a debate raging as to whether all this talk about the different generations is evidence-based or mostly media-driven simplistic categorizing. An article in *People & Strategy Journal* reports on a thorough study done of the peer-reviewed literature on generational differences in two areas:

1. Career Management and Organizational Loyalty
2. Work-related Values and Attitudes

Here is their conclusion:

> *"In sum, our review of 26 peer-reviewed studies found few consistent differences among the generations in the workplace. Only eight of those studies reported some support for generational differences; 18 did not."*

Probing deeper into the eight possibly promising pieces of research, they concluded that none supported differences across all four generational cohorts, some looked only at certain regions or industries, and all were lacking in a sufficiently high "degree of scientific rigor."

So, should managers try to adjust their style when dealing with boomers vs. Gen X & Gen Y? Well, the report suggested that we be on guard for our perceptions of differences (we all are influenced by the popular media).

My cut on this is that, while growing up in different decades can influence what we are good at, how we function in daily life, and what we learn in school, the main thing is we are all human beings–physically, culturally and emotionally. No matter their age, employees struggle with the archetypal human issues of fear, fitting in, power & influence, being valued, and having what they do at work matter.

So, dear bosses, by all means use different communication technology vehicles and chunk your message differently for the different age groups and listen for their different motivators. But lead them, delegate to them, challenge them, give them tough feedback, develop them and respect them in the very same way.

# Having The Tough Performance-Related Conversations

In this competitive and cost sensitive environment organizations are coming face-to-face with an unavoidable truth: they can no longer afford to carry on the payroll people who contribute less than a fully satisfactory job.

Yet dealing with poor performance is one of the toughest tasks a manager is called upon to perform. Furthermore, most managers lack the skills and self-confidence to deliver corrective feedback needed to turn around poor or marginal performers. Hence–being human–managers typically delay or avoid confronting employee performance problems altogether.

When managers do take action on just a few of the weakest performers, it sends a convincing message that the leadership is serious when they talk about "excellence," "quality" and "high performance." At the same time, their action heartens the good performers and boosts overall morale.

The best organizations provide their managers with the skills and support they need to deliver timely, accurate, and assertive feedback, whenever the situation requires.

# Practice Difficult Employee Conversations

Frequently in my management workshops and always in my coaching practice, a manager will bring up a "difficult employee" situation and ask how they can have the tough conversation with that individual. Usually it is about some area where the person is not performing adequately. Sometimes it relates to a negative attitude, a generally lazy work style, or resistance to work assignments.

The challenge in these conversations is to:
1. Keep your cool
2. Listen for how the employee avoids, blames others, or denies any performance shortfall, and
3. Respond assertively so that you move the "monkey" of account-ability over to the employee, where it belongs.


The way some employees deflect responsibility can raise your ire in a heartbeat. You can easily get tangled up in their masterful manipulation which some have honed over the years with past bosses who failed to get them to do what they are paid to do.

The solution is to do dry runs of the conversation. In other words, practice.

When it comes up in a workshop I often ask the manager to engage with me in a short role play of the interaction in front of the class. He/she plays the difficult employee as realistically as possible (and they usually do a very convincing job of it). I play him/her, the manager, and we play out a typical or actual situation. Then, with the help of the class observing, we analyze how successful I was in avoiding the employee's "hooks" and getting him/her to take adult accountability for the job performance in question. We may then replay the scenario with the manager playing himself/herself and me taking on the role of the employee. Training participants frequently report that these magic moments were the high point of learning for them from the entire course.

You can do this role-play technique at work. Ask a trusted peer manager or perhaps your boss to help you out. Have them play the employee and give the interaction a couple of dry runs. If the employee (actor) succeeds in turning the responsibility or blame back on you, analyze what you said (or didn't say) that allowed this to happen. Make corrections and role play it again. Consider even recording the practice rounds in audio or video to help you get a clearer picture of how you are coming across.

One neat by-product of this methodology is that when you take on the persona of your difficult employee in a role play, you actually get a feeling of what it is like for him or her when interacting with you. It takes you to a new level of understanding of what is going on between you two and helps you be more effective dealing with the individual.

I know, it's weird but it works.

# Cause, Not Blame, Produces Better Performance Feedback

I subscribe to Alan Weiss's thought provoking monthly email newsletter called *Balancing Act* (http://summitconsulting.com/databack/index.php). In one issue he offers the following tip:

> *"Here's a quick secret for getting along and playing nicely in the sandbox: When something goes amiss, don't look for guilt, look for cause. Focus on correcting the situation and not blaming anyone. The former develops support, the latter enmity."*

While he mentions it in a more general context of human relations, it is a good reminder for managers whose employee screws up on a task and the situation calls for feedback.

Depending upon the gravity of the situation and the history of the employee involved, it's hard not to swing directly to the blame option. Judgments of the employee as incompetent, uncaring, or even malicious flow into our mind. This just makes us angry, a rather destructive frame-of-mind in which to engage the employee in "constructive" feedback, wouldn't you say?

Operating from a place of anger or frustration activates what author Seth Godin calls our reptile mind, causing us to block out other explanations. We neglect to consider the staffer's skill level (training) or other external forces in play such as lack of resources, too many pressures on the employee, or difficulties in the system of work and information flow.

Blame speaks—not favorably—to the imagined intention of the individual. If it is their fault, why look beyond the person to other possible contributing causes?

We need to program into our minds—yes, we're talking about a mental habit here—a *default response that scans for cause, not blame*, when a staff member falls short of acceptable performance. Your spirit of problem-solving has a chance of turning around performance AND building a more trusting relationship. The other way never will.

# Taking Your People to Where They Don't (Think They) Want to Go

Janice Stein, a political scientist at the University of Toronto, said a key indicator of a successful political leader is that he/she **takes people to a place they don't necessarily want to go**. I like this, on a macro scale. Think Lyndon Johnson on civil rights legislation, Helmut Kohl on embracing the eastern part of Germany after the fall of the Berlin Wall, or Nelson Mandela on healing a nation divided (see the film *Invictus* for a vivid portrayal of the latter).

Now take this concept to the micro level, down to the one-on-one relationship between you (the boss) and one of your employees who happens to be listless, sloppy, and clearly underperforming. You want him to change…to a new way of working: doing the job asked of him (or her). If this individual is, in fact, capable of doing the job well, the problem is one of attitude, of lack of motivation.

The best managers are able to turn around this commitment thing. They:
- Clearly lay out what they expect from their under performer
- Raise for discussion the current gap in his performance
- Express their belief in his ability to do the job well
- Lay out the benefits, to both the employee and the organization, of a solid job performance
- Involve him in identifying the obstacles to his performing better
- Get him (i.e. not the boss) to come up with a plan to turn around his performance
- Reach agreement on the plan, with specific actions, measures and time frames

Going deeper, the manager might probe into what the employee wants from his job, what motivates him, and what's missing for him as a motivator in his current work. All the while, in the background hangs the potential for consequences if the staff member chooses not to change. The leader brings tough love to the situation.

The best bosses foster a mindset of high performance in their unit. They get all of their people to *want* success and *want* to perform at a level of which they can be personally proud. **Almost all of your people want these–success, pride, accomplishment.** When you first confront a poor performer, however, he just doesn't realize that he does.

# Suppress Your Default Response; Listen First

I was doing some small group coaching sessions with members of one of my clients' management team. These sessions were designed to keep alive the learning from a multi-day leadership development program we had delivered earlier. The participants assembled in groups of six-at-a-time for a couple of hours to address specific people-management issues and questions that had arisen for them since the training had taken place.

Small group coaching is a powerful process which generates stimulating, problem-solving discussions. While I facilitate it and inject my perspective and suggestions, so many of the ideas come from the wisdom and experience gathered around the table. In addition, during the course of the conversation opportunities periodically arise for me to engage in an on-the-spot role play with a manager around a specific challenge with an employee.

At the end of one of the sessions, a manager said that she saw a pattern in all of the issues that she and her colleagues had raised in the meeting. She said that every case

> *…involved the manager acting too soon and without sufficient information to deal with the situation in the optimal way.* She went on to say that *we managers aren't listening enough, aren't asking enough questions.*

It was a brilliant summation and I couldn't have agreed with her more. In fact, as I cast my mind over the two other sessions I held that day, this pattern had been present there as well.

Each case involved, at least in part, an employee who was not being forthcoming with the boss about the employee's motivations, needs, opinions, concerns, fears, assumptions, perceptions of their current behavior, reasons for poor performance, etc. For example,

- An employee is bored and unmotivated. The challenge is first to get him to identify what he wants from his work.

- A staff member bickers a lot. The manager has to get her to shift from blaming to expressing what she needs instead, what is missing for her around each complaint.
- An employee believes he walks on water and rates himself a 5 (out of 5) in all areas. The manager must first get him to point to the specific results and/or behavior that he believes he is delivering in his job.

We talked that day about the strong tendency managers have to try too hard and too quickly to "fix" "people problems" by giving advice or direction. As a result, they usually end up pushing their own solution on the employee (boy, don't we all love it when our boss does that?) or solving the wrong problem.

If only, as that manager said, we would first really listen in order to really understand.

# What's Your Ask/Tell Ratio?

Do you ask your employees as often as you tell them what to do and what you think?

But if you are not sure how you would answer this question, I invite you to spend a week or so watching yourself–as a third party would–as you interact daily with your staff.

- If your employee is struggling to collect more accurate data for his weekly status report, do you jump in with your advice or ask what he has tried or what he could try?
- If your employee's performance falls off, do you tell her HOW she has to work differently or do you get her to come up with some ideas?
- When your team meets to discuss a problem like why production is falling, do you offer/impose your opinions or ask them first?
- And when the team comes up with some ideas, do you probe their thinking further or simply acknowledge these and then trump them with your own answers?

I have no scientific data on what the asking-to-telling ratio is for the best bosses but I suspect it lies somewhere between 3-to-1 and 5-to-1.

I wonder what a week of tracking this will yield for you?

# Skills & Knowledge...
# Leveraged through Attitude

At a workshop presented by one of my colleagues, leadership consultant Kevin Shane, he made a point that really resonated with me. Kevin said,

> *"Your attitude has a huge multiplier effect on your skills and knowledge."*

Your employees can have terrific skills and a lifetime of technical knowledge but, unless their attitude is positive, they will fail to apply these toward the best results they can achieve.

As a leader, your skills and knowledge are the price of entry, the starting platform on which to build your effectiveness. Ultimately, however, it is your assumptions, beliefs and habits of thought that will turn you into a truly effective leader and differentiate you from the rest.

For example, you can be a whiz at strategic planning and a hard driver for results. But if your belief about recognizing the performance of others can be summed up by the statement, "The fact you are still on the payroll is your signal that you are doing a good job," your people will not give to you the best they have to contribute.

I regard skills and knowledge as important resources, nothing more. So, when you are trying to turn around an employee's performance or help her achieve more of her potential, spend less time attending to her competency and spend more on her level of commitment.

# Again...Do We Need Performance Appraisals?

Another respected thought leader, this time Stanford University professor and prolific author Jeffrey Pfeffer, has raised the question about the efficacy of the vaunted performance review. In the July 23, 2009 issue of Business Week he lists several of the classic reasons why **rating** an individual's job performance is counter productive (e.g. hard to objectively measure, open to human rater bias, the influence of the employee's innate political skills).

The biggest criticism, says Pfeffer, is that there are numerous system-based variables that can have a significant impact on an employee's performance, variables over which he or she has no control. What resources and information are available to perform the job? What about the quality of the direction from his immediate boss? Did priorities shift in mid-year that redirected his time and attention from his standard job? Does the input arrive late or sloppy from another department on whom he relies to do his own work?

By all means, have frequent conversations, formal and informal, with each of your employees' about their job performance. Share your expectations. Acknowledge when these expectations are and are not being met. Solicit your employee's input and solutions. Problem-solve with him when he is falling short.

But move away from a system that allows you to give him a 2.0% increase instead of 2.5% because you, in your (parent-like) wisdom, rated him as "slightly above satisfactory" instead of "fully above satisfactory." He won't be motivated by this beyond next Friday. He'll probably be demotivated. I would be and so, I'll bet, would you.

I encourage you and your chief human resources professional to take a good look at your performance management process and forms. If you can find a way to eliminate ratings altogether, do so. For some ideas on how to compensate your people without a formal annual rating, check out the thought-provoking book, *Abolishing Performance Appraisals*.

# Latest Findings around Performance Goals and Competencies

Hewitt Associates have come out with another informative study, called The Current State of Performance Management and Career Development 2010. They surveyed HR professionals from 193 employers.

**On the performance side**, they looked at how companies are using performance goals (the "what") and behavioral competencies (the "how") in their year end performance assessment process. Here are several key findings:

While 15% said that their employees' individual performance goals were very **aligned with the company's business strategy**, a full 73% said they were only *somewhat aligned*. The issue is whether you can see a direct line of sight from what an employee works on and the strategic objectives his or her work supports. What would you say for your organization?

- **How many performance goals** do they typically have for an employee? 70% reported 4-6 goals. We at Fulcrum Associates suggest 4-7 Key Result Areas in our own "Aligning Your Unit" process.
- As for reliance on **behavioral competencies**, the vast majority of reporting organizations use competencies that reflect a range of areas, particularly leadership, job specifics, function/skill, and organizational values.
- One constant issue for discussion: **what weight should you give to results vs. behaviors** that get you the results? Not surprisingly, the higher the level in the hierarchy the greater the weight placed on achieving results. In 30% of the firms, performance measures for executives were based solely on results. Other firms reported basing their weightings on various combinations of results and competencies.
- Finally, who engages in what sometimes are called **"calibration meetings?"** These are where managers get together, review collectively, and then make decisions on what the final overall

performance rating will be for each individual employee. From my experience, these meetings are a really good investment of time. They ensure consistency of criteria (e.g. what do we mean by "satisfactory", what's a "3"?) applied to ratings across the organization. At the same time, the management team can discuss possible actions to close an employee's performance gap and suggest priorities for developing a particular individual, going forward. Here's what Hewitt found out about the frequency of calibration meetings:

» 43% hold such meetings and the group makes final decisions.
» 18% hold the meetings but the group only provides for the respective direct managers.
» 39% do not hold calibration meetings.

Food for thought as you look at your own situation. [Note: In the Hewitt study you will find equally interesting points about **career development** but I'm not addressing these here.]

# 4 Steps to Effective Performance Management

The *Institute for Corporate Productivity* recently came out with four recommendations for putting in place an effective, robust process for managing and recognizing individual performance.

Focusing, as is their wont, on the practices of high performing organizations, their research found that:

- Less than 20% of organizations in general have managers who are very highly or at least highly skilled in conducting performance reviews.
- It is critical to managing individual performance effectively that you have the right set of skills resident in your managers and supervisors.
- High performance enterprises are twice as likely as low performing ones to provide training in these critical skill areas;
  - » Developing goals
  - » Giving and receiving feedback
  - » Conducting a performance review meeting

High performers address not only **results** (goals, metrics, etc.) but also the **behavior** that generates the results.

Here, taken verbatim, is their four-part recommendation:

1. **Train managers to deliver effective performance management.** Arming managers with the ability to properly develop goals, give and accept feedback, write up appraisals and provide motivation will greatly improve the overall performance management process. Training on how to actually conduct the appraisal meeting is also critical.

2. **Differentiate and reward top performers appropriately.** Use the performance management process to identify the true superstars in the organization. Then reward those people accordingly. If the top merit increase in your organization is 5%, and the average

employee receives 3.5%, then there really is not much separation and you risk losing top talent.

3. **Address and resolve poor performance.** Simply rewarding high performers and ignoring low performers will not suffice. Similarly, culling the bottom 20% and replacing them would be a costly endeavor. Instead, identify the factors leading to the poor performance. Perhaps there are development opportunities that could help or conflict issues that can be resolved. Given the proper direction, a low performer can often become a high performer. If termination or similar actions are necessary, those decisions are made easier by examining all of the possibilities first.

4. **Encourage continual feedback.** Waiting until the end of the year to tell an employee how they are doing helps neither the high- nor low-performing worker. Low performers never get the course correction they may need to turn things around, and this can lead to an ugly appraisal meeting. High performers also benefit from ongoing feedback. The recognition of work well done can keep them engaged and on track.

These are so sensible. They offer a straight-forward roadmap to follow. If you are a senior leader, be sure to demand, engage in, and support a process that does all four really well. Our training program, *The Skillful Leader*, can deliver on items 1, 3 & 4. Your HR folks can, with your encouraging them, devise a system to see that #2 is installed.

All your employees–most importantly your star performers–will appreciate this and your organization will surely reap the benefits of everybody contributing more.

# Shift–from Evaluation to Coaching

Gary Ridge, CEO of the highly successful company, WD-40 (the lubrication folks) believes that everyone in his firm should get an 'A' in goal achievement.

Their performance management process reflects this emphasis…

- They begin by annually setting individual goals and performance standards (nothing new here)
- They mandate quarterly performance conversations with each employee (nice, but not anything original)
- During these discussions, manager and employee review how the latter is doing against his or her objectives. If the staffer is on target for a goal he/she gets an 'A.' If not, a "B" is noted down. (hmm… starting to sound new)
- But the conversation doesn't stop there. Remember, the intent is for the employee to get an 'A' in every measure.
- A's are acknowledged and celebrated.
- B's are not at all bad, however. Not a whiff of evaluation arises, no comments suggesting a "thumbs down" from the boss. Rather, a 'B' is a trigger to move directly into partnership and problem-solving. The manager asks questions like, "What's getting in the way of an 'A' for you here?" and "What can you do differently? How can I or the organization help?."
- It may mean that the job duties need to be adjusted, or more resources provided, or that the employee needs to apply himself more diligently, or training is needed.
- The accountability of both parties is on the table. (Now we're into "new.")
- The year end performance appraisal at WD-40 they call "reviewing and learning."

Since instituting this system, Ridge reported that annual sales have tripled, from $100 million to more than $339 million. They have a retention rate three times the U.S. national average and consistently register employee engagement scores in the mid-90's (percent).

I really like the non-judgmental flavor of their approach. I like the spirit of *winning*. I like that their conversations around performance adopt an adult-to-adult tone.

If you are interested in reading more, check out the book by Ridge and Ken Blanchard, *Helping People Win at Work*.

# Creating a Motivating Work Environment

Economic conditions and market forces can fluctuate widely, generating fear and discouragement that dampens the enthusiasm of employees and translates into lower morale, reduced output, and poorer quality work. In addition, boredom, burnout, and approaching retirement can sap a worker's will to do a good job.

In all fields and especially in work involving technical/professional knowledge, creative ideas and independent initiative, skills alone will not ensure superior job performance. Employees must also possess the desire to apply their talent, energy, and ideas to achieve strong results.

Each manager plays a critical role in keeping his or her staff intellectually and emotionally connected to what motivates them in their work. But many managers do not realize the positive impact they can have on their employees' motivation to perform, nor do they know how to bring up this issue with their people.

Every manager's training should include an understanding of the impact of a wide range of motivators on employee performance and should include specific skills for helping staff members identify what currently motivates them in their job and career.

# A Lesson for Managers from the World of Sales

By far the single biggest concern I hear from managers I work with is, "How can I get my people to do more?" Their number one challenge is how to ensure their employees are motivated. For the answer to this question we turn to the sales professional.

Superior salespeople do many things well but one thing stands out. They get into the head of their prospect/customer! They start where their customer is—cognitively, emotionally, even physically. How do they do this? By becoming curious—asking questions and listening intently—about their customer's:
- hopes & dreams (what they want)
- fears and concerns (what they don't want)

Our sales star now determines whether his or her product/service provides a solution for the customer, or whether to refer him/her elsewhere. If it does, they proceed to link their solution to the customer's indicated need(s)

Your employees are like your customers. They want things from their work. Let's call these "benefits." Examples are money, recognition, opportunity to learn and advance, balance, and challenge. Avoiding what they don't want is also a benefit to them. For example, a pay cut, being downsized, boredom, stalling in their career.

You are like the salesperson. You are often, though not always, in a position to satisfy their needs. In return, you require their performance contribution.

Sales coach Tom Stoyan calls selling "helping your customer make a buying decision." Managers, encourage your people to articulate what they want from their work. Many are not sure. You may have to facilitate their thinking process: "What do you want?" "Uh, I dunno. More money, I guess." "OK, money. And what else?"

Know that most people will be motivated to perform once they perceive a clear link between their effort and the outcomes they truly value. This is when you make your "sale!"

# What Science Knows about Motivation

The energetic author, Daniel Pink, has a new book. It's called *Drive*: *The Surprising Truth About What Motivates Us*. I did a book review on it. (http://www.888fulcrum.com/review-drive/)

I strongly recommend that you view the 20-minute presentation Pink did earlier this year at the TED conference (http://www.ted.com).

Best bosses know how to create an environment that motivates their people. What Dan Pink nails in this piece is how high performance in 21st century knowledge-based and creative thinking tasks require **intrinsic motivators,** based on on internal desire to do a job well because it is interesting, challenging, causing us to grow, and has a purpose greater than ourselves.

He relegates the traditional carrot-and-stick approach that is still the knee-jerk style of so many of today's managers to only those jobs and tasks that are simple in steps and clear in deliverables.

As Pink says, science already knows this. Business just hasn't caught up. As a result, managers are "leaving on the table" a lot of additional performance for which they are paying but not receiving.

# Behold the Motivational Moose

"Don't they get it?" said the executive, "If we don't generate a good return to our shareholders, there won't be any investment in the company. And, without investments, there won't be any more company to give them their job. What more motivation do they need?"

Do you hear a faint echo of your parents here?

Here is the reality, the "moose (hey, what can I say, I'm from Canada) in the room" when it comes to the subject of employee motivation. What motivates the C-suite occupants in a company just doesn't do it for the rest of the employees. Sure, most of them understand that turning a profit is necessary and, sure, our shareholders need to see a consistent, impressive level of earnings per share.

But achieving these metrics just don't get the average employee's heart going pitty-pat, pitty-pat. It just isn't a motivator! Look instead to *autonomy, mastery*, and *purpose* (Dan Pink) or perhaps *equity, achievement*, and *camaraderie* (David Sirota) for things that do motivate the broad masses of your staff, including your middle managers.

Something happens to managers when they ascend to high levels in a company. They find their interests and attention now hitched to the same metrics that the investment industry pays attention to. They forget that people below them in the enterprise are engaged by things other than quarterly financial results.

Accept it, executive, the moose is waiting for you to acknowledge its presence.

# Look Beyond the Money for Their True Motivators

In PwC Saratoga's latest Global CEO Survey, 65% of CEO's report that they intend to *use more non-financial rewards to motivate their staff.* This is an admission that the a motivation strategy full of mostly financial reward "carrots" is not enough, especially for their highly skilled and high potential employees.

We so easily forget the fact that people are looking for at least some measure of **fulfillment** from the time they spend on the job. "Fulfillment," of course, can take many forms: interesting work, challenging assignments, variety, freedom to make decisions, the opportunity to serve, making a difference in the lives of others, growth and learning, developing and mastering new skills, camaraderie, and so forth.

Fulfillment is not primarily about money. Tami Simon, CEO and Founder of Sounds True, (http://www.soundstrue.com/shop/Welcome. do;jsessionid=XasX0ATarrIxPocR38YS.app01) puts it eloquently:

> *"The scaffolding of a workplace that is defined by people leaving their souls behind and coming in in order to make something called "money" so that they can squeak out a little time where they can have soulful lives is an absurd tragedy. That scaffolding needs to be taken down and not bought into."*

What motivates your employees to contribute fully is deeper and more complex than you (and they, for that matter) realize. In conversation with each one of your staff members, probe for their motivators, the ones beyond money. Do everything you can, within the constraints of their job and the room you have to maneuver, to see that they experience fulfillment…whatever that means to them.

# One Employee at a Time

Back in the 90's the Royal Bank of Canada had a series of TV commercials touting the theme, "Building a Better Bank, One Customer at a Time." The message, as I recall, was that RBC treats each customer as a unique individual and strives to win them over, one-at-a-time.

I frequently refer to this ad campaign in my management development workshops. (http://www.888fulcrum.com/services/workshops/) The parallels are natural…

- RBC has customers, current and new. Managers have employees, current and newly hired.
- RBC seeks to understand the individual needs of each customer and then find a way to satisfy them. The best managers learn what their employees want from working and, in return for good performance, try hard to satisfy this.
- Customers who are treated as individuals and given good service will become customers that stay and continue to bring their business to the bank. Employees who feel cared about and whose needs are met from their job are employees who remain fully engaged and deliver solid performance.
- Finally, RBC customers who are treated this way will reinforce the message by telling other RBC customers and prospective customers. Employees who are treated this way will tell other employees and overall loyalty to the employer will go up.

The lesson for managers is to really get to know your staff, what they are looking for in their job, and what they aspire to down the road. Periodically, check in on how your people are doing, whether they are still satisfied and engaged, and if there is any way you (the manager) can help them be more successful in performing their job.

Your employees are different. They have different personalities. Each one is unique. Each responds to specific motivators and these shift over time.

The best bosses win their team members' loyalty, engagement, and retention one employee at at time!

# Oh Yeah, That's Why We Do This Work

I have been working lately with an organization that serves the homeless population by first finding them a place to live and then helping them attend to the many needs of everyday life. As with many non-profit enterprises these days, they have their share of frustrations that can tip staff morale down a notch or three: lack of broad based funding streams, coping with the whims and delays of government support, attracting and keeping good front line people who can work effectively with their destitute clients, and so forth.

Recently a client of theirs who had been ailing and in declining health passed away. A couple of the managers stayed with him in a death vigil that ended in the early hours of the morning. The community based team responsible for this client had been his surrogate family. It was a special privilege, a manager said, to be present, supporting him at the moment he passed on.

The following morning the team met for awhile to work through their feelings in what was a grieving session…like any family would need to do following the death of a loved one.

What struck me was something one of the managers told me. "Going through this experience reminded us of how vital is the service we provide. Remembering a moment like this helps me put up with all the daily struggles I encounter doing this work."

I hope you never have occasion to experience the deep emotional impact of easing one of your clients out of this world, but you certainly can get back in touch with the mission of the work you have chosen, no matter how menial or ordinary your job may seem.

# (Re)Frame their Job as Something that Matters

Richard Florida is a provocative thinker around social and economic issues. He first became noticed from his book, *The Rise of the Creative Class*. In his latest book, *The Great Reset*, he shares data that the future growth of jobs will be in two areas: (1) knowledge, professional and creative jobs and (2) lower paying, more routine work in the service sector.

Citing progressive companies like Wegman's, Whole Foods, REI, Zappos, Nordstrom, and The Container Store, his thesis is that work in the services industry in fact offers potential to provide workers a space for innovation, ideas, and some degree of individual entrepreneurship within the job.

He implies that most service jobs can be *fulfilling*. He asserts that, as a society, we have no choice, "we can't give up on service jobs," we have to find a way to manifest the potential for employee engagement and intrinsic job satisfaction in service work. I agree with this.

Now it's over to you, managers in the service sector! It falls mostly on your shoulders to make this happen. No one is better positioned to reframe service work as being:
- about the person(s) served by the employee and not the work itself
- about the benefits the employee's efforts provide to others (the "customers," regardless of whether they are external or internal)
- about "service" in its most honorable sense, helping your fellow man (and woman) even in a very small way.

So, you tell the staff of your fast food outlet that their work is not cranking out Whoppers, fries and a Coke. That's drudgery. The work is about providing a friendly, positive **experience** for the people in line, quick access to a meal, a short respite from their hectic day, and for those who dine in, an opportunity for them to connect with their dining partner(s).

# A Neat Approach to Employee Recognition

Elsewhere in this book ("Marketing Your Core Messages–Internally") I talk about the remarkable success B.F. Saul's Hotel Division has had internally branding it core operational values.

There's one other nifty element in their story that I want to mention. They have come up with an innovative way to reinforce the importance of learning and, at the same time, let their staff do the teaching.

It's simple, yet brilliant. **It's a desk calendar.**

Each year they produce a new calendar with a different theme. For example, the theme in 2010 was "lifelong learning." They sent a number of focus questions out to their entire employee group and invite people to send in their responses. Here are some of the questions for that year's calendar, along with a smattering of responses they garnered:

What life lesson would you like to leave behind to teach others?
- Step back from the immediate picture.
- Pay attention in math class!
- There is always the other side of the story.


What have you learned from your children?
- That sleepovers are a contradiction…no one actually sleeps!
- Sometimes children have a more simple approach and tend to not confuse the issues.
- Have fun in life.


What's the best lesson you ever learned from your mother or father?
- Daily give and you will never run out of things to give.
- Education and manners help you go far in life.
- Measure twice…cut once. You can apply this to just about everything in life.

What have you done to better yourself personally or professionally during your adult years?
- Learned about health and fitness
- Become a better listener.

Who was your favorite teacher and why?
- It's OK to fail and the importance of asking the right questions.
- The importance of humility and respect.

Whom in life do you consider to be your mentor and why?
- My dog: He loves me no matter what, forgives me without confession, and lets me hug him anytime.

What one thing would you still like to learn before you die?
- Spanish, piano, and ballroom dancing.
- Make better food.

What terrific questions! They encourage people to be introspective. They draw from the past but also focus attention forward. They shine the light on the value of lifelong learning.

On each of the 365 days in the year, a gem of wisdom from a different employee greets staff members who turn the page of their own calendars and start their new day.

I love how this both honors employees and recognizes the knowledge about life they bring to their workplace.

# In Their Play, You Are Only a Supporting Actor

Brian Hayman, one of our associates at Fulcrum Associates, has penned some wisdom that I would like to quote:

> *"We write stories for ourselves in which we cast ourselves in leading roles and assign supporting parts and cameo appearances to others. It's their job to love and admire us, promote and give us raises, laugh at our jokes and take our side against our enemies, figure out our needs and satisfy them.*
>
> *At some point, however, when we go public with our imaginings and raise the curtains on our plays, we find that we are sharing the stage with 6.5 billion other leading men, women and children who have cast us in supporting roles and given us cameo appearances in their stories."*

It is so easy to forget that, even though you are the boss and focus on higher level challenges and larger responsibilities, in your employees' version of the "drama" you share you with them are not the star. They are! While they want you and the unit to succeed, **the core theme in their "play" is that they get what they want.**

In my leadership development workshops I frequently field complaints about staff who don't care enough about the fortunes of the unit or the company. These employees aren't sufficiently jazzed about the bottom line or the new product launch, or about finding ways to work more productively. From the perspective of the manager, the supporting cast isn't supporting enough ("Don't they know their role? Haven't they learned their lines?").

My advice is to these managers is to remember that in the employee version of the play called "My Job" the boss does not have top billing and the organization/office/job site is but the stage upon which the employee's personal saga unfolds.

How do you engage this employee leading man (or woman) since, in their play, it's first and foremost about them?

Decide what you want them to treat as important and then actively link it to what is important to them, to their expressed needs and concerns, and even to their sense higher purpose and spirit of contribution.

We're all employees. It's not that we are self-centered prima donnas concerned only about our personal gain. It's just that, when the credits roll, our name appears at the top and we naturally expect that to mean something special.

# Being a Leader is All about the Group

Professor Alex Haslam of the University of Exeter, in a presentation put on by the Canadian Institute for Advanced Research, took the following position in answer to the question, "What makes a great leader?"

> *"The traditional models [of leadership] are built around an "I-based" model of identity, where the individual's personality is so strong that others cleave to the leader out of sheer inspiration and loyalty.*
>
> *The truth is, though, that the most effective leaders draw on a "we-based" collective identity–followers see their leader as "one of us." It is group identity, not a single person, that makes or breaks the leader. In fact, to really understand what makes an effective leader, we also have to understand what makes a dedicated follower."*

I think the good professor raises an overlooked factor of successful leaders. *Without a group of followers with needs, you have no need for a leader.* And, for managers, if your employees do not see you as articulating and embodying their interests and needs–vs. just the organization's interests– you will at best be a mediocre manager who will have to drive compliance among your staff to produce, at best, mediocre results.

In the context Haslam presents, I think there are three things a manager must be sensitive to, talk about, and support in his or her behavior and actions:

1. What each *individual* employee wants, needs, and is motivated by
2. A sense of the identity and pride of the "tribe" (i.e. the unit, department, function, region, etc.)
3. The shared vision–what we are all together trying to achieve and contribute…to people beyond the group (i.e. What are we creating and for whom are we creating it?)

The so called "great man/woman" approach assumes that the leader motivates followers *solely* through his or her own vision, courage, charisma, knowledge and intelligence. If, however, you can tap into the three elements above that are of interest and inspiration to your team, you will stand out from those managers think that their success is all about themselves.

# Getting Motivated by Meeting those You Serve

It's notoriously hard to motivate people who work in repetitive or routine administrative or blue collar jobs. Adam Grant, management professor at the Wharton School of Business, however, has done some research which perhaps makes the task a tad easier.

*Knowledge@Wharton* reports on a series of experiments by Grant, (http://knowledge.wharton.upenn.edu/article.cfm?articleid=2436)     all linked to the idea that if you have the opportunity to meet, face-to-face, with at least a sample of the people who ultimately benefit from the work you do, your performance level will rise.

- In a **fundraising call center**, reps who had met a few of the recipients of the funds were more persistent, spending significantly more time on the phone, and secured significantly more donation money.
- **Lifeguards** who read case studies of people whose lives had been saved by the actions of other lifeguards increased the hours worked and were rated higher by their supervisors on helping behavior.
- **Individuals at a Career Center** editing the resumés of job seekers, if they had even just a brief chat with the applicants, spent much more time on the task.

Adam Grant summarizes the results: Employees who know, first hand, how their work impacts others in a positive and meaningful way are happier than those who don't and are vastly more productive.

He goes on to point out that this dynamic holds equally for employees whose work product serves internal "customers" (end users).

Think of your work flow and administration processes in your organization and whom your unit serves. Food for thought…

# Have Your Employees Take a Fresh Look at their Jobs

So many people–some studies put the number as high as 50%–are not happy in their current their job. Almost all of these, I reckon, believe that their job is cast in concrete, that it can't be changed. In fact that's not true, for the vast majority of jobs.

Are you looking for new ways to help your employees boost their level of engagement and motivation in their work? Here's a process (and accompanying tool) you may want to check out. It's called **"Job Crafting."** What it enables your employees to do is take a fresh look at their job duties and priorities and better align them with their:

- **Motives** – outcomes they would like to obtain (for them and for others) from their work
- **Strengths** – their natural skills, attributes, talents, etc.
- **Passions** – activities and areas of their job that they most enjoy or find the most interesting

Information on the Job Crafting methodology is available at the *University of Michigan's Center for Positive Organizational Scholarship*. You can even download a preview copy of the exercise. (note changes) (http://www.bus.umich.edu/Positive/CPOS/Teaching/job-crafting. html) It was reported in a recent issue of *Time Magazine*.

What I like about this approach (and others like it) is:
1. It empowers the employee to take accountability for rendering his or her job more satisfying.
2. The outcome will usually lead to greater job motivation for that employee, simply as a result of looking at his/her job in a new light.
3. The manager can play a coaching role helping the employee work through the process.

Most managers with whom I work feel challenged to come up with new ways to make work more engaging and motivating for their staff, ways that don't require spending more money.

If you are in this group, take a look at Job Crafting.

# The UN Has Them, Why Not You?

David Neeleman, when CEO of Jet Blue, had three principles by which they ran the company:
1. Flawless execution in everything that touches the customer.
2. Make it right with the customer.
3. Treat employees so well that they become ambassadors of the company's brand.

Let's take a closer look at that third one.

There are at least *four good reasons* that are trotted out as arguments for attending to the well-being and for meeting the needs of your employees. I agree with all of them:
1. Leads to greater productivity
2. Reduces staff turnover
3. Keeps high potential leadership talent in the pipeline
4. Increases employee resilience in tough times

We should add Neeleman's ambassador concept as a fifth reason, one that most results-oriented leaders overlook. Employees who see the value they contribute through their work and who have opportunities to do their best work, to challenge themselves to grow and be better will feel pride in themselves. Add in a management group that genuinely cares about them and shows it. Now you have the makings of an "ambassador."

So, what do these ambassadors do for your enterprise? They talk with friends, family and strangers about their job and their employer in positive ways. They become walking testimonials for why people should do business with your firm and why people should apply to work for your firm.

So, if the first four reasons aren't enough to get you to invest in the skills and the development of your managers (I can't imagine why they wouldn't), then perhaps the impact of tens/hundreds/thousands (pick your number) of employee emissaries out there promoting your firm in a very good light will sway you.

# Does Job Satisfaction Lead to Better Results?

This question has been studied for decades and no direct relationship has been established. Despite what would seem to be a slam-dunk connection, happier workers don't necessarily result in a bumped up bottom line.

A recent study by researchers at Cornell, (http://digitalcommons.ilr. cornell.edu/cahrs_researchlink/9/) however, has mapped a path between the two. It is not a direct route. There are three intervening variables:

**Increased workforce satisfaction =**

**Better employee retention + Better employee responsiveness =**

**Higher customer satisfaction > Direct effect on bottom line**

Keep in mind, this was done in a U.S. nation-wide retail company with close to 800 stores. As the researchers admit, the link between satisfaction and results may well be stronger in industries where the interaction between staff and customers/clients is more involved and complex (e.g. professional services) or where design and manufacturing processes require employees to collaborate well.

So, while satisfied staff is a very important ingredient for business success, we can't stop there. Managers need to pay attention as well to (1) retaining employees longer in order to develop their knowledge and experience, (2) how responsive they are to those they serve, and (3) ongoing measures of customer satisfaction.

And how the manager operates has a critical impact on how much each of these key factors are in play in the organization.

# Fostering a Culture of Accountability

We operate in a short-term, fast-moving, problem-responding work environment. Managers can no longer afford the luxury of constantly monitoring and checking up on the performance of their personnel. The cost of this has become prohibitive, both in terms of management time consumed and the continuing drag of a dependent mindset on the part of staff.

Organizations need employees they can count on to meet their job performance commitments and take greater responsibility for their own level of work quality and job satisfaction. Hence, employers are grappling with how to foster a culture of personal accountability at all levels of the enterprise.

This means teaching managers to establish high expectations while, at the same time, prompting their employees to make decisions more independently and solve problems that come up in their work.

It also means shifting the mindset of employees from having to perform to one of choosing to meet or exceed the performance levels that come with their position.

# Choice & Accountability: The Bedrock Of Superior Performance

So, you want to be a success? And you want those who work for you to succeed? Then you might as well know the (bad ?) news. Successful, effective people are courageous people!

Aristotle said courage is the primary human virtue. And the ultimate courage is to accept what philosopher Peter Koestenbaum calls life's "dirty little secret"—that we are all free to choose. We are all free to decide what we desire, how we act, how we feel and who we are.

Many poor-to-moderate performers I see in organizations simply refuse to accept accountability for their job and career. Ask them what they want—besides more money—in their job or how satisfied they are with their current performance and they come up with fuzzy answers or none at all. This does not surprise me. If they were clear, they would have to admit to the choices they are making in their job.

Employees who refuse accountability cost our organizations a bundle. Precious time and energy shifts from productive work to holding on to the old ways, blaming other people or circumstances, doing unquestioningly whatever the boss wants, and avoiding confrontations or any risk. ("Hey, why should I do anything extra? It won't matter to them, anyway.")

Furthermore, when you believe you have no control—that is, no choice—over your fate at work, you feel angry and resentful. Someone else, or perhaps fate itself, is calling the shots for you. This resentment gets expressed, usually through negative comments, barely satisfactory work and/or withholding important information, ideas, effort and enthusiasm.

How can you take on personal accountability at work? Here are three suggestions.

1. **Identify all your "customers" and what they expect from you.** Your key customer is your boss. Don't wait. Ask for his or her performance expectations for you. Approach other internal and external customers the same way. Check in periodically on how you are doing in their eyes.

2. **Decide on the performance level you want to achieve.** Unless impossible, it should exceed others' expectations. Verbally commit to deliver this performance to your "customers". Stay focused on priorities that move you to these goals.

3. **Where appropriate, own up to undelivered performance.** Don't blame others. Solicit and be open to feedback from others. Thank them for their advice and learn from it. Focus on what you will do differently the next time.

Individual accountability offers an extremely powerful leverage point for increasing human productivity. Embrace it. Challenge your people to as well. Think and act as if you are in business for yourself, with an open-ended contract with a single client (your employer).

Watch your performance, confidence and impact soar as you live out the words of poet William Ernest Henley: "I am the master of my fate and the captain of my soul."

# Make it Safe to Take the Risk

In a workshop I was conducting on *Interaction Styles*. I had the group working collectively at a case problem to solve. There was a lot of information and idea sharing and a lot of cross-talk, some of it in sub-groups around the table. At times it became rather chaotic and the effectiveness of the group's process dipped. Nevertheless, they persevered and managed to complete it accurately just as allotted time expired.

During the facilitated debrief discussion an interesting issue emerged. One woman said that, when the process seemed to hit its highest point of chaos, she sorely wanted to get up, grab a marker, approach the flip chart, and start leading her colleagues by capturing what they were saying and organizing it into a coherent strategy to solve the problem more quickly.

I asked her, "Why didn't you do that?" She replied, "Because I didn't want them to think I was being too controlling. I wanted them to see me as a team player."

Notice the assumption she had made about how they would perceive her well-intentioned act to contribute her particular strength (organizing) to the success of the group effort.

I turned to the group and asked them, "If she had stepped up and done this, (1) would you have seen it as controlling and not being a team player and (2) would it have helped you solve the problem faster than you did?" They all agreed that they would have appreciated, not resented or judged, her action and that it would indeed have helped them perform better.

This was what we in the training field call a "teachable moment." From the debrief discussion, the woman who had hesitated to step forward in the exercise learned to question her assumptions and, when her spirit of intent is genuine, to take the risk of contributing where she has a skill. The group learned the importance of making it OK (i.e. safe) for individual members to step forward and take such risks. Both innovative thinking and improved group performance requires this way of thinking.

Do your staff know that you will support them when they bring their particular skills and perspectives forward to propose an idea or a better way to proceed? You may think you have but don't assume that they have received the message.

# The Truth that Hurts but Will Help Us Cope

Managers have been sorely challenged recently to keep optimistic and not succumb to the ongoing, sometimes mind-numbing stress of work and, at best, tenuous job security. They are called to do this not only for themselves but also for their people. One place employees look for assurance that things will be OK is their immediate boss. If she is sounding scared or negative, staff will pick it up too.

But lingering somewhere in the back of our minds is the idea that when this is all over and we all have jobs back again, things will return to how it was before derivative financing and house prices tanked.

Well, it looks more and more like things won't!

**Newsweek Magazine** featured an excerpt from Author Greg Easterbrook's latest book, *Sonic Boom*. In it he talks about the frenetic pace of change due to globalization and how, once we come out of the recession, this will sweep us all back into its vortex, resulting in both benefit and pain. Let me quote him on the bad news part of our future:

*"…just as favorable economic and social trends are likely to resume, many problems that have characterized recent decades are likely to get worse, too.*

*Job instability, economic insecurity, a sense of turmoil, the fear that when things seem good a hammer is about to fall—these are also part of the larger trend. As world economies become ever more linked by computers, job stress will become a 24/7 affair. Frequent shakeups in industries will cause increasing uncertainty."*

I think this means managers must consciously shift the context of the conversations they have with their employees. We need to create a new consciousness about how…

1. We really mean it this time—there really won't be that elusive thing we call security as we go forward in the decade.

2. This means that each one of us, manager and employee alike, needs to start seeing ourselves as what William Bridges calls "You & Company." We have take personal responsibility for our job performance record, our skill and educational development, and our ability to stay marketable in the crazy economy coming at us.

We have to get it ourselves! And we owe it to our employees to drive the message home to them as well.

# What Meets Your Employee's Expectations?

What is the OK norm performance level where you work? Is it "Fully Satisfactory," Meets Expectations," or perhaps "Achieved all objectives?"

And if 70-80% of staff is force fit into this level by the miracle of the bell shaped curve, regardless of their raw performance, maybe it should read, "Good but not good enough to beat the top 15%." Maybe this fully acceptable level is regarded as a good thing at your organization. Or, perhaps it is seen really as only the bare minimum .

Sometimes management sets the bar on performance. Sometimes the employee(s) have input on it as well. However it is done in your organization, I think there is an even more powerful and intriguing question for you to **ask each employee:**

*"What level of performance will meet **your** expectations?"*

That's what I call in my management training workshops a "monkey toss," inviting the employee to take the "monkey" of accountability and identify what she wants to achieve. It sends a message to the employee that you regard her as an active partner in the whole process of defining and monitoring her job performance. Furthermore, psychology tells us that people are much more inclined to commit to achieving goals that they themselves set than to ones laid out by the boss.

Now, I know what you are thinking. What if my employee suggests a goal below what I need from the job?

You don't have to give up your expectation or start hard bargaining for somewhere in between the two targets. You can still ultimately insist on the performance standards you seek. But first have a discussion about why your higher level is necessary and what her concerns are about committing to it. Probe for whether she lacks the will or the confidence here.

Won't it be interesting to hear what your employees each comes up with? You will learn scads about the individual just from her response.

# You Own Half of the Relationship

A post on John Baldoni's *Leadership at Work* blog presented an intriguing image: your "ownership" of the relationship you have with your boss:

> *"To me it comes down to a simple proposition:* **exert your ownership***. If your boss is not giving you feedback, ask for it. If your teammates are driving you crazy, talk to them. If you are struggling with an impossible workload, find ways to lighten it. Proceeding as you are is inefficient; failing to address the problem may be even worse. Bottom line, you have a responsibility to do the job for which you are paid. Do it."*

Actually, you and your manager are co-owners of the relationship. And by "relationship" I mean how the two of you operate, communicate, and treat one another. Isn't it odd that because your boss is at a higher level and has the ultimate decision authority in most areas of the work it seems as if he/she has a greater stake in the relationship. Perhaps as much as 70% to your 30%.

But we are not talking here about power, just about a relationship between two human beings. And this human relationship belongs as much to you as it does to your manager.

So, to expand on John's exhortation, demonstrate the courage to:

1. Bring it up for discussion when the relationship isn't working for you (i.e. when it is negatively impacting your ability to do your job well and/or your sense of well-being at work)
2. Ask yourself what you can do, from your end of the relationship, to remedy or at least improve how you two interact.
3. Ask your boss what he/she needs more or less of from you to enhance how you two interact.

If you owned something essential that someone else was damaging or restricting, wouldn't you take some sort of action? Wouldn't you bring it up with them or even confront them, if necessary.

So, if your current relationship with your boss–the most essential working relationship you are in–is less than you want it to be, what are you waiting for?

# Resist the Temptation to Tell... Ask Instead

In a *Business Week* article entitled *Leadership: How to Ask the Right Questions*, (businessweek.com/managing/content/sep2009/ca20090929_639660. htm) coaching expert Gary Cohen makes the statement:

> *"Before getting into answer mode, ask "Whose decision is it?" If it is your decision to make (based upon your job description), ask questions that will help you arrive at the best answer. If it's your co-worker's decision to make, ask questions to help him or her–referencing his or her particular skills and tendencies."*

What a great filter–*Whose decision is it?*–for a manager just about to open his/her mouth and

EITHER tell an employee what to do to solve a problem

OR get the staffer to come up with a solution.

Pretty well all managers who attend my leadership workshops, when faced with this decision in a case role-play about an employee's poor performance, default to telling, not asking. It's comical to watch it happen. Advice streams out of the (person playing the) manager's mouth before they realize what they have done. Then they look at me, smile, smack their forehead with the palm of their hand and say, "Man, I just did it again, didn't I?"

This is a huge lesson for managers to learn because they are working against synaptic pathways worn deep over years of giving their employees the answers.

So, the next time you sense you're about to inform an employee of what he or she should do, swallow that golden piece of advice and ask yourself Gary's question, "Whose decision is this, anyway?"

# TW 2010 Global Workforce Study – Comment #1

TowersWatson's 2010 *Global Workforce Study* (http://www.towerswat-son.com/global-workforce-study/) covered 20,000 full time employees of large and midsize organizations in 22 markets around the globe. I want to highlight and comment on some of their main findings. My focus is on what the learnings are for managers and leaders.

Three main themes emerged:
1. The global recession has permanently altered the so-called "con-tract" between employees and their employers.
2. There is a gap between what employees want and what employers are able to provide them.
3. This is a pivotal time when employers have the opportunity to identify and put in place a more flexible, sustainable "deal" for their staff…before the economy takes off again and we see a flood of unhappy employees packing their bags for greener pastures.

Not surprisingly, the downturn has had an impact on the results in this particular year's report but it did uncover a couple of dilemmas:
- Employees want security above all else (76% of respondents) but only 51% believe it is attainable.
- People continue to hunker down in their current employment, putting a stable job above the siren call of career opportunity. 81% are not actively looking for other jobs, despite the fact that 48% see no potential advancement in their current job.

Here's the news for leaders and managers. Confidence of employees in their managers' interpersonal and relational (vs. operational) competence is alarmingly low…
- Only 38% think their leaders are sincerely interested in their well-being

- Only 47% see their leaders as trustworthy
- Just 42% say that their leaders inspire and engage them
- 53% question whether their managers have time for the people aspects of their job
- 61% question doubt their managers' effectiveness in dealing with poor performers.

Clearly we have a woeful shortfall in the people side of leading at all managerial levels. But despite these numbers, TW sees this time as one of great opportunity for employers:

> *"We are at the earliest stages of a **significant workplace transformation** that will profoundly affect how businesses approach people management and how individuals approach the workplace."*

# TW 2010 Global Workforce Study – Comment #2

A major discovery that emerges from the survey is around **Self-Reliance**. *Three quarters of respondents agreed that they are ultimately responsible for their financial and career security.* This is a good thing. It indicates a tacit willingness on the part of staff to accept accountability.

This invites two key questions for employers, to quote TW…

> *"How much responsibility and risk can reasonably be shifted to employees without impeding their productivity?*
>
> *And what can organizations do to equip individuals to be more self-reliant in owning and managing their own performance, career, financial security, health and well-being?"*

A core teaching in our management development programs at Fulcrum Associates is around how to get your employees to accept the "monkey of accountability" for their performance, career direction and job satisfaction. I am heartened to see our focus corroborated so clearly in TowersWatson's research.

Here's what employer organizations need to do:
- Provide their managers with skills training in how to talk effectively with their employees about their performance (good, bad, or OK) and address their level of job satisfaction, should it falter.
- Ensure that all managers engage their employees periodically in a provocative conversation about their career prospects, what they want, what's required of them to make this happen, and what they can start doing now to mitigate the impact of future economic downturns or a shift in job demand.
- Encourage managers to be a "pygmalion" to their employees by emphasizing the employee's current strengths, assessing his or her potential (no matter how small) and expressing a belief in the staff member's ability to achieve that potential.

- Make training available on personal financial management
- Promote health, fitness and wellness with initiatives such as learning programs, gym memberships, coaching in fitness and nutrition, etc.

These actions certainly fall within the core of that "significant workplace transformation" that TW referred to (see my TW Comment #1) in their study.

# TW 2010 Global Workforce Study – Comment #3

The final finding from the TowersWatson data on which I want to shine a light has to do with treating each employee individually with respect to the constellation of attitudes, needs and motivators they bring to their job.

Quoting the study,

> *"One of the most striking findings from this year's study is the variability in attitudes and expectations across the workforce. We saw differences in why people join or leave organizations, how they define a career, how much risk they are comfortable taking on, what motivates them to give maximum discretionary effort, what they expect in terms of their reward package and what they want from their managers.*
>
> *We found interesting differences among employee segments, for instance, in terms of their relative emphasis on skill building versus wealth accumulation and how that emphasis shifts back and forth in importance across an employee's working life."*

This strongly suggests two things to managers:
1. Endeavor to learn what specifically is important to and motivates each one of your employees, individually. Yes, that means a separate one-on-one conversation with each staff member.
2. Keep in mind that their various needs and the level of priority of these needs can change over time. So, you have to keep checking back in with your people on this every year or two.

Oh yes, and when you query them on this stuff, don't forget to raise some version of the question, "What do you need from me to enable you to be successful in your work?"

Earlier I mentioned TW's finding that employees–at least in this tough economy–want security above all else. They suggested that you distinguish between:

- *Passive* security – the "take care of me" type
- *Active* security – the "equip me to do it myself" variety


We all know that you can't provide the first kind of security any more, even though a ton of dependent-minded employees believe you can... and desperately want you to.

That leaves the other kind of security–"*Active*." This will require a huge shift in the consciousness of the majority of employees out there. Many, of course, will not make the shift. They are not yet at a stage in their own adult development to begin to take on responsibility for their well-being in all its many facets (financial, marketability, attitudinal, performance capabilities, etc.).

The only course of action for you as a manager is to be striving always to get your staff to see the futility of relying on their current employer, current skill set and current effort (or lack of effort) to develop themselves. Challenge them to become the "master of their fate" or at least to do a lot more in that direction.

No one other than you will confront them on this. No one other than them can make the courageous choice to take charge of their own security.

# Developing Leadership Talent

Leadership pipeline strategies are popping up everywhere as a way for organizations to prepare for the inevitable retirement of older managers and the coming shortage of solid talent to backfill key management positions.

Such "pipes" typically expose employees with strong growth potential to a variety of functional roles and geographic locations, ultimately leading to positions of broader responsibility and greater complexity.

In order to successfully ascend, however, emerging leaders must develop a deep awareness not only of their current style and its impact but, even more importantly, of their assumptions and habits of thought that determine how they actually function and how they lead others.

Such development involves much more than simply enhancing their people management skills. It includes inculcating in them a willingness to solicit feedback and confront patterns of behavior that are preventing them from reaching their full potential as a leader.

# Leadership Lessons from the Top 20 Corporations

In the Hay Group's *6th Annual Best Companies for Leadership* study. (http://www.haygroup.com/BestCompaniesForLeadership/research-and-findings/global-top-20.aspx) the top 20 are major corporations with a global presence. Collectively, over the last five years, they have generated shareholder returns that are 36 times better than those from the Standard & Poor 500 companies.

It is worth noting the overall conclusion from the survey:

> *"The Top 20 Best Companies for Leadership are at the forefront of a significant shift away from hierarchical organizational operating models. Leadership in the twenty-first century is about leading at all levels; not restricting it to title."*

While the survey covers a lot of ground, including elements like diversity, HQ/regional office relations, work/life balance, and collaboration required across a global enterprise, I want to isolate **four findings that speak to all managers**, regardless of their organization's size, sector, or industry.

I think these four pieces of data serve as both a reminder and an inspiration for all managers at all levels in all sizes of organizations. <u>Note</u>: The percentages compare the top 20 with the rest of the organizations Hay surveyed.

1. Everyone at every level has the opportunity to develop and practice the capabilities needed to lead others. (100% vs. 69%)
2. Leaders in my organization create a work climate that motivates employees to do their best. (100% vs.68%)
3. Our leaders personally spend time actively developing others. (96% vs. 56%)
4. There are a sufficient number of qualified internal candidates who are ready to assume open leadership positions at all levels in my organization. (100% vs. 55%)

These best companies are clearly ones that see "leadership" as permeating potentially every nook and cranny of the firm and not restricted to people with formal titles like manager or supervisor.

They see two key roles of their managers to be:

1. Foster motivated staff (dare we call this "self-leadership?" Yes, I think we dare.)
2. Dedicate some precious time to personally attend to developing and coaching their employees.

And they regard having a pipeline of ready or emerging leaders to be a core strategic element for their continuing impressive business growth.

**What these four elements do is unleash the tremendous potential within your staff.** Of course, you can adopt them in your small or medium sized organization too. A pipeline in a small firm can be as simple as succession plans in place for the critical management positions. Managers can be given–and measured on–a key result area to attend to the individual development of their people, coming up with assignments and projects that will stretch them, and coaching them along the way. In addition, progressive management training integrated into the mix will show your managers how to bring out the very best in their people.

If you are not emulating the Top 20 where you work, what are you waiting for?

# At the Core of Developing Our Leaders

In their wonderful (nay, more than wonderful–exciting–if you are into leadership development) new book, *Immunity to Change*, Robert Kegan and Lisa Lahey lay out three easy-to-understand levels (which they call "minds") of adult mental development. These represent plateaus of human maturation that encompass 99% of our population. While they are a distillation of more complex models of human development that include up to seven or eight levels, these three are all we need when looking to advance today's crop of leaders in our organizations.

1.  **The Socialized Mind**

    These individuals are true *followers* who just want to know the rules, the job duties, and what they are supposed to do. Their behavior is shaped by what is expected of them by important (i.e. more powerful) people in their world. They live their personal and work lives based on clear beliefs and ideologies usually handed to them by authority figures they've known or institutions they have attended. They make good team players and loyal followers. Roughly 20% of the population is at this stage or striving to attain it.

2.  **The Self-Authoring Mind**

    These people have their own agenda and goals and they push hard to achieve them. They are guided by their own values and personal codes, rather than just accepting the expectations of others. They are not afraid to take firm stands. They drive themselves with a focus and work to get others to buy in to their goals. Research puts about 75% of people at or on the way to this level.

3.  **The Self-Transforming Mind**

    While living a focused and purpose-driven lives, these people have the ability to step back and see the impact of their beliefs and goals in a wider context, especially in relation to stakeholders who have a different version of what is true, real and right. And they are open to considering the limitations of their own perceptions, assumptions, values and personal ideology. In fact, they pretty well assume that their perceptions fall short of the full truth of any situation.

Many managers you know are operating more at the *socialized* mind level of leadership. They believe it is their job to ensure that their employees conform to corporate policies, rules, conventions, job descriptions, etc. They don't have a particular idea of what they want to be better in their unit, preferring either to clone last year or to implement whatever vision their boss has put forward. If they did have an agenda or vision for their unit, it would be evidence of upgrading their mental "operating system" to the *self-authoring* level.

Much of the work I do in training and coaching managers involves helping them to operate fully from a *self-authoring* mindset ("What do **you** want to be different in your operation in 12 months time?" "What do **you** want your unit to accomplish this year?"). The rest of the time I am inviting them to get curious about the pieces of the "truth" that their employees and others bring to any discussion or decision to be made, especially when these perspectives differ from the manager's own assumptions about reality and what's best.

What's really interesting to me is that our ascent from *socialized* through *self-authoring* toward *self-transforming* involves having more of our personal experience in life shift from "subject" (what we do/believe unconsciously) to "object" (what we now recognize consciously, in other words, what we can **observe ourselves doing and feeling** in our interactions with others.)

I, as your boss, may be having a heated argument about a task I want you to do. You are resisting me. All I see across from me is a "stubborn" employee who, furthermore, is "willfully shirking his/her job responsibility." In fact, I am making judgments about you with out realizing it. All I am aware of is my anger toward you. Immersed in my frustration, I pull rank and tell you, "Just do it, dammit." I am operating at the level somewhere between the *Self-Authorizing Mind and the Socialized Mind*–I have clear, demanding work standards for you and, besides, the "rules" say that the boss gets his way. By resisting me, **you** are breaking the rules.

Instead of letting my blood pressure go through the roof, however, what if I were to at least explore what's behind your resistance? What if

I became curious about your point-of-view, realizing that this will (1) show respect for you, even though you are resisting me, and (2) enable me to make a better management decision around your performance? By taking this approach, I will have taken a first-step up to the *Self-Transforming Mind*.

This is a prime arena for leadership development today. It's where we at Fulcrum Associates have decided to focus our leadership development efforts. I invite you to consider what it can mean for your own growth and that of the managers in your organization.

# The Four Strategic HR Challenges for the Upcoming Decade

Boston Consulting Group, in conjunction with an association of people management associations worldwide, completed a comprehensive on-line + live interviews study on how they are approaching strategic human capital development for the next decade. It's called "Creating People Advantage 2010" (http://www.bcg.com/documents/file61338.pdf) and worth downloading if you are concerned with the strategic element of human resources in your organization.

Among a wide-ranging group of topics, their results address how human resources challenges have been changing in the last few years. As a manager, you should find this interesting.

The four (of 21 potential challenges) that were ranked at the top are:
1. Managing Talent
2. Improving Leadership Development
3. Strategic Workforce Planning
4. Enhancing Employee Engagement


Globally and in Canada they were rated in the above sequence. In the US, numbers 1 & 2 were reversed. What causes these four to be high leverage areas of focus are that they are rated HIGH on *future importance to the success of the enterprise* and LOW on participating organizations' *current capability do deliver* on them.

Equally intriguing is how the rankings have changed over the last two years of economic hell (from a BCG earlier study in 2008). While numbers 1 & 2 were unchanged, the next three challenges back then were *delivering on recruiting, managing work-life balance, and managing change and cultural transformation*. Remember when these were the hot topics?

Executives' continuing concern for talent development and ensuring a pipeline of superior leaders reflects the increasing complexity of the environments in which we all operate. Plus, of course, the fact that, baby boomers will–yes, someday relatively soon–be retiring.

The fourth ranked HR strategic challenge, *Employee engagement*, is now on the C-suite radar because of two factors:
- First, employees for the last two years have:
- been pushed to do more and work longer hours
- had their salaries frozen or lowered
- been left in a state of constant uncertainty about their own fate
- been deprived of learning and growth opportunities.


Many, most importantly the best employees, are stressed, discouraged, and not happy with their current employer.

Second is the realization that it is not sufficient just to put in place enough of the right people in the right jobs at the right time. If we are to reap the full return on our investment in our staff, we need to ensure that they are highly engaged. Despite Woody Allen's famous line, 90% of success is NOT just showing up.

There is a lot in the BCG report to prompt important strategic questions for managers and leaders of even small organizations, including those in the not-for-profit and public sectors.

# Executive Coaching: On The Rise

Isn't it funny what we assume about leaders in senior positions. They no longer have anything to learn about interpersonal relationships or leadership. They have arrived, proof positive of their skill level!

Furthermore, only a fearless few people will give them the honest, useful feedback that self-development requires. The "culture" expects them to be role models and our models are supposed to get it "right." Showing their vulnerabilities is a "no-no," not to be done in front of those who report to them and certainly not advised in front of competitive colleagues on their leadership team. Of course, the CEO is too busy (and often not sufficiently skilled) to help them grow interpersonally.

The fact is that many individuals arrive at the senior level with much still to learn about people. Often they bring to the executive wing styles, habits and beliefs that have worked for them since they were a supervisor. Suddenly these formulae for success no longer work and, in many cases, must be unlearned and replaced with behaviors more in line with modern leadership.

This is why so many organizations today are investing in coaching for their key leaders. The benefits from being coached stem primarily from the leverage that is obtained. When a senior leader operates with a less-than-functional style, its negative impact on performance and morale can reverberate from within the senior leadership team right out through the frontlines to the customer. The good news is that turning this individual's style around will have the same multiplier effect in a positive direction.

## What is Coaching?

Coaching is a series of periodic one-on-one consultations, usually with an external resource, over a period of time—typically anywhere from three to eighteen months. Between sessions the "coachee" (whom we will call the "client") applies newly learned approaches at work, receives feedback, then reassesses, and refines his/her behavior accordingly. Coaching is not therapy, however, occasionally a coach may suggest counseling as a promising course of action for deeper seated issues that are blocking effectiveness. Well done coaching yields a high return on investment because the process is totally customized to the "client's" challenges and needs and it maximizes the executive's time off the job.

The goal of the coaching process is to generate, in the client, effective skills and attitudes that are self-sustaining, self-correcting and directly supportive of his or her expected performance results.

## When does one engage a coach?

Usually—but not always—it is the individual's boss who initiates the coaching intervention. Typically this is in response to a need to turn around a significant performance problem or to improve an interpersonal skill deficiency that is holding back an otherwise excellent executive. Coaching is also used to prepare someone for a promotion, generally enhance leadership potential, and provide support for a particularly challenging leadership situation (e.g. managing a major change, inheriting a new department).

On the other hand, Coaching is not always indicated. I would not take on a coaching assignment when the boss has already decided to fire or demote the individual, when there is insufficient time to generate the results required, or where the person is entering a coaching process against his/her will. This latter condition is sometimes a judgment call but my ethical and business bottom-line is that the client must buy in to the process freely and genuinely.

## What should you look for in a coach?

Consider the mix of (1) skills, (2) knowledge and (3) attributes of any coaching consultant.

Critical skills are:
- communications (interviewing, listening, feedback, summarizing)
- facilitation (including the ability both to confront and support)

- teaching
- the ability to take a systems perspective (the client does not operate in isolation but as an integral part of complex organizational systems)

Look for knowledge in three areas:
- psychology and human behavior
- business, management and organizational life
- how adults learn

The ideal attributes include:
- flexibility
- work experience and maturity
- self-confidence
- confidentiality
- comfort with complexity
- ambiguity

I believe your coach should be someone who places a high value on—even has a passion for—the growth of others and who is willing to learn and grow himself/herself in the process. And, of course, the relationship must work for both parties, client and coach.

Some coaches are clinically trained, that is, they are psychologists or professional therapists. This is not necessary but neither is it negative. Clinicians bring a deep understanding of human behavior and effective interpersonal techniques. They are trained to recognize deeper pathology should it become evident during the process. As long as they have a solid understanding of business and organizations and they stick to coaching, certainly do consider them for coaching.

# What does a coaching process look like?

Each intervention is unique but let's look briefly at a typical sequence:

1. Coach meets with the client's boss and the client to ascertain issues, objectives and the standards expected by the organization.

2. Coach and client meet. In this meeting I particularly check out our chemistry and my client's degree of buy-in to the overall process. Once that is confirmed, I conduct an in-depth interview with him/her to scope in detail his/her personal and work background, version of the issues, feelings, needs, concerns, and how the client currently perceives and interprets his/her world.

3. Data gathering. This may involve interviews with key players in the team, the client's direct reports, and others who interact with him/her. Often a 360 degree feedback instrument is used to obtain perceptions from the client's boss, peers, and subordinates. Psychological measurements also can contribute a lot. I routinely use the Myers-Briggs Type Indicator© with great success. Another technique is to "shadow" the client and observe him/her in typical interactions and meetings.

4. Coach compiles all this information, feeds it back to the client, and facilitates a discussion—sometimes lengthy and emotional.

5. Client identifies and commits to specific objectives and deliverables for the process.

6. Client develops an action plan.

7. With the on-going involvement of the coach, the client implements the plan over an appropriate number of months. This is the core of the process.

8. Once the plan has been accomplished, client and coach conduct a final assessment of the client's progress against the objectives. Here we may determine the need to gather data once again to confirm others' perceptions and experience of the progress made.

9. Finally, a ninth step might be contracted where the coach checks in occasionally over the next year or so to provide on-going support.

When we look to the world of athletics and entertainment we see that those who aspire to excellence understand the value of coaches. The seasoned masters in my field of professional speaking certainly use them. I have several coaching colleagues amongst whom we coach one another.

What about your key people? What about you?

# Leadership Coaching Has Really Arrived

A recent article on Workforce.com (http://www.workforce.com/archive/feature/training-development/boom-business-coaching/index.php) report summarizes a study on the prevalence and impact of coaching on the results that individual managers generate. The research surveyed CEO's, HR Managers and other executives at over a thousand US and international companies, roughly 40% of which had more than 1000 employees and over $500 million in revenue.

Here are a few of their findings:
- 52% of companies currently have business coaching programs in place and 37% plan on adding such programs in the future.
- The demand for coaching is being driven by the impending talent shortage when the baby boomer cohort starts retiring.
- Coaching works!
  » Companies with coaching programs report strength around revenue growth, market share, profitability and customer satisfaction.
  » Managers who have been coached are more likely to set work-related goals and have their leadership abilities trusted by their staff.

Organizations can reap a healthy payback on their investment in coaching when it is targeted at:
1. Executives
2. High-potential employees
3. Key employees who can contribute high technical/functional value but are challenged by dysfunctional attitudes and poor interpersonal or leadership skills.

It makes sense that coaching works because it offers a scalpel approach when behaviors, attitudes, and habits of thought must be changed to make an already key employee make their full contribution to the enterprise.

And the coaching process is pretty darn effective at getting the client to lock in the new behavior/thinking patterns!

# Is the Coaching Client Ready?

James Prochaska and Carlo DiClemente (University of Rhode Island) developed a *Stages of Change Model* that for 30 years has helped therapists and counsellors work effectively with clients with addiction. Here are the six stages:

1. **Precontemplation** (not yet acknowledging a need for changed behavior)
2. **Contemplation** (acknowledging the need but not yet willing to proceed with the change)
3. **Preparation/Determination** (ready to make the change and gearing up for it)
4. **Action** (engaging in the new behavior)
5. **Maintenance** (sustaining the new behavior over the long term, hopefully permanently)
6. **Relapse** (returning to the old ways)

What intrigues me here, in the context of executive coaching, are Stages 1 & 2.

Obviously, a manager will not grow to greater leadership effectiveness if he or she doesn't:

- see a problem with how he/she is operating currently, or
- have a genuine desire to become better.

Coaching is an investment made mostly in senior managers or identified high potential future leaders. So, as you look at potential candidates in which to invest your limited development resources, the first question is to clarify is to whether they are currently at the *Precontemplation* or Contemplation stages.

If they are not, below are several ways to move them through to stage 3. Through these strategies you will raise an individual's conscious awareness that he/she has a problem or perhaps some untapped potential.

- Express your belief that they have potential to rise to a senior

leadership role in the organization. (Note: this is by no means a promise. You are just informing them of your perception.)
- Administer a 360° feedback process for them to give them a reality check on how they are currently being experienced by others.
- Challenge them as to what their own goals and career aspirations are.
- And, for less-than-acceptable performers, give them clear, tough feedback about their current poor performance and the consequences if they don't turn this around.


The final step before you decide to invest in someone is to solicit to what extent he/she is willing to do the tough personal and professional developmental work in order to make a shift to greater effectiveness.

Absent that **genuine** willingness, don't waste you money on coaching.

# How Should We Help People Learn Leadership?

A close associate of mine, Brian Hayman, heads up a leadership training firm called *Getting in the Groove (www.gettinginthegroove.com)*. What's remarkable and really cool about their programs is that they always feature a live improvisational jazz combo. I want to share a couple ideas triggered for me from a particular "Random Riff" blog post Brian wrote exploring the comment from an executive that, while *he didn't believe that leadership could be taught, he did believe it could be learned.*

One thing Brian raises is the importance of questions (from the learner) in the learning process. If he is to grow, especially in such a complex competency as leadership, the learner must be continually curious about what he hasn't yet mastered, about how he could have better handled a leadership situation. And curiosity is all about *questions*. But Brian goes on to say that equally important is the *timing* of the questions. They have to come before the answers are given. In fact they have to drive the search for answers. The emergence of questions indicates that the learner is ready to move ahead and in what area of the skill he seeks to know more.

So, in the spirit of a learner, I find myself raising a question, the one in the title of this piece, in fact. Of course, individuals have many preferred learning styles. For example, some like to learn on the job, by doing, by trying it out. Others like to observe the skill in action before trying it out. Yet others prefer first to learn the theory, to understand the concepts behind the thing being learned, then take a crack at it.

Whatever style your people prefer in learning to be a better boss, I agree with Brian. Every individual's leadership development process has to be learner-directed. This means the manager has to resist the temptation to tell the learner how to be better **before** she even realizes that her current style could be improved upon. And then she still needs to be willing to learn. Otherwise, as Brian points out, you are giving your employee the answer before she has come up with the question.

Here are a few thoughts on what managers, mentors, coaches and trainers of budding leaders can do for learners, while being careful to honor the "question" issue:

- Watch for when they are struggling or when they experience a setback or fail to handle a situation well. These offer potential teachable moments, opportunities for them to step up, reflect on what they did, and open themselves to potential new, more effective ways of responding as a leader.
- Don't give feedback about their improvement unless they ask for it. You might, however, offer to discuss it *if they want to*. (e.g. "Would you like to talk about what happened?")
- Alternatively, regarding their struggling or their setback, ask them how they could have handled it differently or what they plan to do the next time a similar situation arises.
- If they are performing below what is expected, however, do remind them firmly of the performance goal, confirm that they are committed to achieving it within a specified time frame, and then ask how they plan to meet the target.
- Consider taking a "pygmalion" approach as their boss where, based on their strengths and track record, you express your (genuine) belief that they are capable of achieving greater accomplishments. The key is to put your observation out there and let them pick up on it or ignore it. Trust that, if there is a part of them that in fact would like to grow and access more of their potential, they will come back to you with, guess what…their questions.
- Build a leadership development program in your organization that offers a mix of:
  - » classroom training
  - » individual reflection
  - » employee involvement in setting learning goals
  - » planned on-the-job learning and application
  - » special project or task assignments
  - » one-on-one support coaching or mentoring
  - » some reading related to leadership
  - » regular follow up regarding their progress.

In sales, questions from a prospective customer are known as "buying signals," indications that the prospect has at least some interest in your product or service but harbors some concerns that must be met before they will be ready to proceed to a sale. An effective salesperson satisfies their prospect's concerns while expressing their (genuine) belief in the ability of the of the product/service to meet the customer's needs. As Canadian professional sales coach Tom Stoyan says, the role of the sales professional is to *help the customer make a buying decision.*

It is no different in building leadership capacity in your organization. The professional manager role is not to teach people how to be leaders. Rather it is to help them learn.

# Looking for Leadership in ALL the Right Places

I began my career in the airline industry. I hit a spell when I was languishing in an uninspiring job, wasn't growing, and truth-be-told, wasn't trying very hard to change things. As a diversion, I was drawn into Toastmasters, became deeply involved in their public speaking education program and moved into leadership positions in my local TM club. I also found myself organizing an international table tennis tournament for airline employees.

These were outlets for my leadership learning to blossom. Looking back, I should have channeled this energy back into my career but, hey, I was young and naive. It seemed easier to make a leadership mark in a volunteer capacity. Furthermore, it was self-affirming, a lot of fun, and I received recognition for my efforts.

Leadership development, aka talent development and high potential ("HiPo") development, is a hot issue, particularly in the private sector. The best organizations are always on the lookout within their ranks for potential future leaders. And at least the larger firms have formal processes for identifying these folks.

But how do you know that you have a future star in your department, especially if the work you have for them doesn't provide an opportunity to lead others?

Listen for what your people do outside of work. With some, you'll be pleasantly surprised—and impressed. Are they running a community baseball league? Organizing a 10K run for some worthy cause? Chairing a committee in a non-profit organization?

Now your challenge, as their manager, is to find ways for this enthusiasm to manifest itself in the workplace. What a loss if it doesn't.

# Leaders Master Results
# AND Relationships

The research evidence continues to trickle in. The study I write about today was conducted by Green Peak Partners with the involvement of Cornell's Industrial and Labor Relations School (my graduate alma mater, as it happens). (http://greenpeakpartners.com/resources/pdf/GreenPeakCommentary.pdf)

They did in-depth interviews of 72 executives from 31 companies, comparing elements of their people skills with the business results they achieved. To summarize the results, J.P. Flaum, the managing partner of Green Peak, said:

> *"Our findings directly challenge the conventional view that "drive for results at all costs" is the right approach. **The executives most likely to deliver good bottom-line results are actually self-aware leaders who are especially good at working with individuals and in teams**."*

Here are a few key findings:
- The hard-driving, results focused style, without concomitant attention paid to interpersonal relationships, will work only in very short-term crisis situations. Beyond that, such leaders perform badly on all key financial metrics, including growth, profitability, and ROI.
- Add in strong leadership skills to a results focused style, however, and an executive performs very well.
- Self awareness is a primary driver of an executive's overall effectiveness.

Strong interpersonal/leadership/team skills, however, is not the same as being "nice." It includes being tough and demanding and frank in feedback, when necessary. But it also includes treating employees at all times with the respect they deserve as adults and human beings.

This data, combined with other recent research (The Leadership Circle, Zenger Folkman, and others) is why we offer *The Authentic Leader* (http://www.888fulcrum.com/leadership-programs/the-authentic-leader) program for C-level managers. And it's why we spend time, even in our mid-level manager training program, on the assumptions, beliefs, and habits of thought that determine so much how a manager operates on the job.

# Not Only Purchasing Will be Effected

A *Newsweek* magazine article entitled *The Richer Sex* reminds us of the rapidly growing purchasing power of women around the planet and how some (but not enough, and that's the point of the article) companies are tailoring their products and services to appeal to the female customer. If the current trend continues, the author writes, "the average woman will make more than the average man by 2024."

Put aside for the moment flex time, work life balance, glass ceilings and mommy tracks. The fact remains that women are rising in influence and numbers with the ranks of management in our organizations, including the many that are being founded by the fairer sex.

This trend promises to bring more of the type of leadership skills we need in this post-modern economy: teamwork, collaboration, dialogue, relationship building, and treating employees as "thou's" not "it's." In my workshops and presentations on leadership I notice more concurrence and head-nodding from women in the room when I talk about such people-centric approaches.

It's not the whole picture, obviously. We still need managers who can be tough, deal with conflict, push for stretch results and the like. But when you combine these with an ability to engage your employees as the whole human beings they are, you become a "best boss ever."

For this reason I am heartened by the trend.

# The Last 10%

Awhile back Seth Godin wrote a blog post about how our true expertise and professionalism is reflected when we do what's needed to be one of the best, in that top 10% of people who do the work we do. But it doesn't come easy. As Seth says:

> *"The hard part is the last ten percent, sure, or even the last one percent, but it's the hard part because everyone is busy doing the easy part already."*

Studies by Jack Zenger and his crew reveal that managers above the 90th percentile in terms of leadership effectiveness achieve significantly higher results in areas such as commitment, thinking about quitting/leaving, satisfaction with pay, net income, turnover...need I go on?

In fact, however, very few of the managers I meet in the course of leading management development workshops and keynoting on leadership are trying to enter the top 10%–even 20%–of managers. How about you? Have you considered setting a goal to be a truly extraordinary manager? And, is your organization giving high priority to this across its management and supervisory cadres?

The payoff is there. I just wish more business owners and C-suite executives would realize it. Making a serious investment in the quality of your managers may not constitute the absolutely "lowest hanging fruit" for growing your revenue. But is the longest lasting and the most competitiveness-enhancing and, therefore, the sweetest.

# It Pays to Attend to Your Organization's Talent

The Hackett Group completed a 3-year Talent Management Performance study (http://www.thehackettgroup.com/tmmaturity/ MarketingResearch10keyFindingsTMML.pdf) that showed how Global 1000 level companies that invest in and develop more comprehensive talent management capabilities yield benefits in three areas. They call it the "triple payoff":

1. Enhanced bottom line results
2. Improved operational processes
3. Better talent management processes

Here are just a couple of highlights from their research. Compared to their peer companies, these firms, which they called *Talent Management Maturity Leaders* (TMML's), experienced:

- Earnings (EBIDTA) 18% higher
- Net Profit Margins 54% higher
- Greater retention of staff, in particular those coveted high performing employees
- Higher levels of business & operational process efficiencies

TMML companies engaged in more comprehensive workforce development, management & leadership development, and succession planning. They tracked key metrics around staff retention and engagement. Notably, they didn't leave talent management up to the HR department. Rather, TMML's approached this key strategic component as a joint initiative involving HR, line managers, and the top team.

Hackett defines "talent management" as:

> *"…the activities by which organizations identify talent needs and acquire, develop, manage and measure talent."*

You don't have to be a big corporation, however, to attend to the talent of that strategic resource called "people." Nor do you have to be a big corporation to reap the many benefits when you do.

# A Gap in Your Senior Leadership Bench Strength

The baby boomer cohort (commonly accepted age range: 46-64) are the proverbial pig-in-the-python, demographically speaking. Economists raise the alarm of a looming shortage of workers when the "pig" has passed on through. But is this true for executive and senior leaders? There is no shortage of warm bodies to move up to the C suite. But, says a joint study by Pearson and Executive Development Associates entitled *2009/2010 Trends in Executive Development*, unless employers start to act now, there will be a shortage of people who are fully **prepared** to operate at an executive level.

The research reveals a mixed picture with respect to those managers who show general potential to move into the top level over the next 3-5 years. On the plus side, they have high integrity, ability to deliver results and manage multiple operational priorities, and strong technical skills and knowledge.

However, current senior executives surveyed said there is a serious gap in two critical areas:
1. **Critical Thinking** (strategic perspective, ability to create a vision, a system understanding of the enterprise, ability to shift back and forth from big picture thinking to operational and tactical issues)
2. **Motivating and Influencing Others** (leading change, inspiring and engaging employees)


These both involve complex constellations of competencies, the first are cognitive and the second emotional/relational. They take time to develop but here are three things you can start doing immediately:
1. Put a comprehensive leadership development program and process in place. This includes combining formal and informal on-the-job development, coaching, and training. At the same time, establish some form of leadership pipeline and succession strategy that feeds ready talent onto your future executive bench.

2. Give your high potential managers real opportunities to tackle the kinds of business issues that are fuzzy, with many non-quantifiable variables and with no clearly superior solution. Whether they succeed, fail or do just OK on these, what they will learn about themselves, mixing metrics with intuition and involving the wisdom of others, will be invaluable in mastering Critical Thinking.

3. Develop their emotional intelligence. This includes the ability to build relationships with employees, boss, peers, customers, and key others within and without the enterprise, listening, managing feelings (theirs and others'), enrolling and exciting others about the vision, etc.

Bonnie Hagemann, Executive Development Associates' CEO said,

"The results of this research, combined with the current demographic shift in the workplace, should be a *wake-up call* (emphasis added) for any organization that is not focused on developing tomorrow's leaders."

Is your top team still asleep when it come to your future bench strength?

# Attend to the Pipeline

Despite the bump (yes, in the long term, it's a bump) of the extreme slowdown that started back in 2008, we are still facing the demographic truth that a lot of boomers will be retiring from the active workforce over the next decade. As enterprises across the planet begin to grow again and the excess of unemployed and underemployed workers has been absorbed, we will be back facing a shortage of talented people.

Therefore, in order to put in place the quality and quantity of leaders you will require to expand in this environment, you not only need to hire the right people and retain them. You will need to rapidly develop leadership talent and avoid bottlenecks in what management expert Ram Charan and others have termed the "leadership pipeline."

Here are a few things to consider to build an effective "pipeline" through which to grow and deliver the quality leadership talent you need when you need it:

**Talent management.** An array of strategies that involves attracting the right mix of skills and potential, fostering employee engagement & retention, and building the leadership capacity of managers and potential managers.

**Succession planning.** A comprehensive schema for identifying the mix of skills and experience required for the different leadership levels (Charan's book, *The Leadership Pipeline*, is excellent on this), where the organization's current and anticipated skill gaps exist, and a plan to bridge the gap.

**360° assessment & feedback.** A survey instrument to acquire input from all directions (i.e. 360°)–boss, peers, employees, and self–on an individual leader's style, behaviors, and (I strongly recommend) habitual thought patterns that underlie those behaviors. Undergoing an updated 360° every few years helps a leader immensely to target the investment of time, effort and money toward areas that promise the greatest increase in his/her overall leadership effectiveness.

**Leadership development programs.** Elements such as classroom training, on-the-job coaching and mentoring, one-on-one work with an external coach, on-line learning, special project assignments, and individual reading and reflection can be combined for a customized strategy to develop leadership competencies.

Oh yes, and do check out *The Leadership Pipeline*.

# A High Risk Strategy... Build Your Top Leaders

*The Wall Street Journal* recently had an intriguing article, entitled "How to Keep Your Best Executives." (http://online.wsj.com/article/SB10001 42405297020394690457430201 1865406286.html) In it the authors report on research that says executives are attracted by three particular opportunities, all of which serve to build up their marketability in the job market. These are the opportunity to:
1. Take on greater responsibility
2. Broaden their skills
3. Cultivate a network of influential relationships


What intrigued me about this is the ironic contrast between how a company operates in its marketplace and how it operates with its key executives. While, on the one hand, a firm might boldly adopt an aggressive business growth strategy and take some calculated risks, at the very same time it may be timid, internally, in how it treats its executives and senior managers.

Being bold internally means, as the article suggests, (1) continuing to invest in your executives and senior managers in ways that build their ability to leave you while (2) being sufficiently confident that you can make your organization a very desirable workplace where they will want to continue to work long after the recession has lifted.

Another irony, the very fact that you help your key people become more employable will be a major determining factor in their decision to stay.

This, of course, calls for guts and self confidence on the part of CEO's. The WSJ article throws down the gauntlet, challenging them to demonstrate that boldness with the very people they rely on.

# Up and Down...between the Balcony and the Dance Floor

Ron Heifetz and his co-authors, in their excellent book, T*he Practice of Adaptive Leadership*, presented this vivid and easy-to-remember visual image which they apply to the process of leadership development.

Imagine you are down on a dance floor, dancing, obviously. While you are in the midst of the dance, moving in close rhythm with your partner and with people swirling all around you, your vision is restricted in two significant ways:

1. You can't see the big picture of what's going on across the entire floor and how effectively and smoothly you are in flow with the other dancers.
2. You are so focused on what you are doing, moment to moment, that you haven't the time or opportunity to reflect on your performance.

Now, imagine you leave the floor and go up to a balcony overlooking the dance. Now you can see the big picture and reflect on how you were doing and what you need do in order to be more effective tripping the light fantastic down there.

So it is, say the authors, with leaders who seek to enhance their ability to make an impact on their unit and organization. They need to continually be shifting their focus, over time, from the floor to the balcony and back again.

I've just run across this again, in Henry Mintzberg's great new book, *Managing*. His conclusion is that the practice of management is so complex, such a tapestry of roles, influences, contexts, personal energy, level of character development and interplay with countless others that it can't be taught in an MBA program, let alone in a short classroom workshop. In fact, he says, management can't be *taught* by anyone! The individual must learn primarily through his or her own efforts. To quote Mintzberg,

*"It is through the interplay of reflecting and acting that managers strive for synthesis. Managers work not only work deductively and cerebrally, from reflection to action… They also work inductively and insightfully, from action to reflection."*

**So what does this mean–practically–for you and the managers you want to develop?** Here are a few of my thoughts:

- Most shifts toward greater mastery of people management come from experiences (successes and failures, positive and painful) and approaches and techniques we try out **on the job.** (the dance floor)
- This learning in the crucible of our job can be augmented periodically by *classroom training* (balcony), to focus on acquiring and practicing skills in specific areas on which we need to focus.
- *Coaching* (balcony), either from an external coach, from the immediate boss, or from a mentor, is great for targeting a few critical skills and helping the manager delve into them in depth.
- 360° feedback assessments (balcony), often done in conjunction with one-on-one coaching, can generate extremely useful data on which to reflect. Out of it can come significant change in both behavior and attitude (dance floor).
- Focused discussions (balcony) among managers, either in a structured *group coaching sessions* or informal get-togethers (e.g. monthly, over lunch) are a powerful way to build learning. Here managers, exchange ideas, best practices, tips, and techniques, as well as lessons learned and things definitely not to do, and reflect on how each of them can improve as a manager.
- The best way to leverage time and money invested in training or coaching is to have the manager return to work (dance floor) and consciously apply a newly acquired approach or skill and then assess (balcony) how well it worked and how it could be tweaked to be even better.

For this reason, we at Fulcrum Associates are building more ways to support, back on the job, the learning people take away from our leadership development programs. These include:

- follow-up monthly reinforcer emails to the participants
- post session teleseminars or webinars
- structured conversations, pre- and post-program, between the participants and their respective managers
- facilitated small group coaching sessions where participants bring their current issues, questions and people management challenges and this forms the agenda of the discussions.

What has worked for you or where you work?

# Leadership Development... Even in Tough Times

Hewitt Associates has published once again the bi-annual study they have lead since 2002, *Top Companies of Leaders*. They narrowed down over 500 entries to the top 25 North American companies and top lists globally.

The finding most intriguing to me is that **these top enterprises are still investing in the development of leaders with the same discipline and single-minded purpose as in previous, better economic times.**

Some highlights in this regard:
- They see leadership development as a critical business strategy.
- They focus on programs that demonstrate proven impact on leadership effectiveness and business results.
- Their leadership and talent development strategies are aligned and executed against organizational goals and strategic priorities.
- Large majorities of them maintain robust formal succession plans and attend to the talent at every stage of their leadership pipeline.
- 360° feedback assessments play an important part of their development processes.
- The reputation of the top companies for leadership is strong.


So, what is your organization doing about developing your managers and leaders these days? Are your initiatives all on hold, pending better days? If so, do you know something that the major companies don't?

Or maybe not…

# Breaking News! People Aren't Things

One of my favorite quotes that gets at the essence of leadership comes from **Stephen Covey**. I often open with it in my leadership workshops and keynotes:

> *"You can't "lead" things. You can't lead inventories, cash flow and costs. You can't lead information, time structures, processes, facilities and tools. You have to manage them.*
>
> *Why? Because things don't have the freedom to choose. Only people do.*
>
> *So, you lead (empower) people. You manage and control things. The problem is, the organizational legacy we've all inherited says you do need to manage and control people."*

Now, isn't this simply the nub of it all?

To start with, it's in our psychological DNA, as humans, to want to control–manage–our immediate environment. That includes the people with whom we come into contact. **Add to this** the expectation of companies that managers control their departments. That includes their employees. **Add to this** that most managers started their careers in a professional, technical or hands-on capacity where it was their job to manage "things" (e.g. deliveries, numbers, data processed, hamburgers flipped).

Our biggest obstacle to being their "best boss ever" is our default need to control our employees–what they do, how they do it, the attitude they bring into the workplace, and their level of job satisfaction. We must **let go** of this need and realize that we can't make them do anything or feel any particular way or be satisfied and keen. Until we do, we will never ascend to that level of effectiveness that we read about in all those best seller leadership books. For some managers, letting this go becomes a life-long journey and some never succeed in it.

A large focus of our management and leadership programs at Fulcrum Associates is teaching participating managers how to engage, challenge and inspire their employees, rather than how to "get" staff to perform and feel positive about their job and the organization.

Are you still clutching on to the need—and responsibility—to control your people? Consider, if you will, gradually relaxing your grip and opening up to a way of leading that really gets results.

# Don't Clone Yourself

A boss of mine early on in my career had a tough, almost bulldog, style. He was a pragmatic, no nonsense guy. He didn't have a wide vocabulary and didn't spend a lot of time talking about concepts. He was super loyal to the company and even more so to the branch of which he was a part. In short, he was the antithesis of yours truly.

I never understood why he hired me, with my Masters degree in HR Management and my parallel interest in the bigger picture and broader developments in the field.

So, one day I dropped my self into a chair in his office and asked him.

> *"Ray, I've always been curious about something. Why did you decide to hire me? We think so differently. You see things in more black and white terms. You act decisively and you are not at all intimidated by conflict. I see everything in shades of grey. I'm tentative and want more time to analyze an opportunity before moving on it. And I approach conflict reluctantly, at best."*

He looked at me with a wry smile and said, "There's your answer, Ian. I don't want another me. I need the different perspective you bring." As a penny dropped in my brain, I could feel the *greening of Ian* happening in real time. His was not a revolutionary strategy by any means, but it was new to me. I also learned that this relatively rough hewn man carried a lot of wisdom inside him.

There is a great line in the wonderful new book, *Being the Boss*. "You want someone who fits in—whose basic values and interest mirror the team's—but not someone who simply blends in." Ray and I were in accord and shared the same values regarding our function (HR), how you deliver the service professionally, and how HR contributes to the success of the business. In that sense, I "fitted in" to his unit team.

But I did not blend in like a clone of Ray would. And, although I recall that he was frequently impatient with my different perspective and approach to the work, he genuinely valued what I brought to the team and to him personally. You know, we were stronger because of it.

# People Still Need the Basics

It amazes me how often when considering a leadership development initiative, a prospective client will ask us for "something new."

They will say, "Oh, we did the Myers-Briggs before. Haven't you got something newer?" Or, "Communications skills, that's much too basic for our managers." I once had a prospect company that put a huge leadership training program out to tender, selected our company, and then proceeded to tell us they wanted something "more sophisticated." This was learning material, mind you, that had worked successfully with (quite sophisticated, thank you very much) mid-level and senior managers in numerous other organizations.

If you are charged with selecting development programs, particularly in *human interaction* areas, be careful that your own level of knowledge and mastery of the skills to be taught doesn't blind you to what your trainees really need. I encounter this particularly with Human Resource professionals and well-read line managers. They have attended all the conferences, heard all the latest gurus, taken all the feedback assessments and instruments, learned all the latest concepts and jargon, read all the books by Tom Peters, Pat Lencioni, John Maxwell, Stephen Covey,…

The fact is most of your managers who came up through professional, technical, administrative, sales, and blue collar labor streams often have not been exposed to even the more well-known approaches and skills of leadership. Instead, they have been busy honing their functional, specialized knowledge, skills, and craft.

Don't be afraid to deliver the fundamentals around people management. Your people still need to master the "blocking and tackling" of management: listening, using questions, setting expectations, delivering feedback, handling conflict, articulating a vision, motivating employees, managing priorities, confronting poor performers, etc. It may be old material to you. You may be a seasoned savant in these areas but most of your managers have a good way to go yet before they master these skills.

The classic management and leadership skills are, in fact, archetypal success skills for the human species. Now, if we had the privilege of working with a group of your experienced managers, we may present some of these at a deeper level and demand more from the group. But the topics are the same.

Take **listening**, for example.

- You can learn how to listen to someone and minimize your attention drifting while you do. That's at the basic level.
- At a deeper level, you can listen for what's not said or gestured but might still be part of the person's deeper message and feelings.
- At yet a deeper level, you can listen to what's going on inside you as you receive the other person's message.

Any one of these skill levels could be taught under the same title, "Mastering Listening Skills."

So, don't be seduced by the latest "in" thing around leadership and management. Look at what your target managers really need to get the results you want in your organization. Even if they have been exposed to a particular skill before, how well do they demonstrate it? Could they benefit from either a refresher or a more advanced application of this competency?

Exemplars in any field never stop revisiting and practicing the basics.

# Leading High Performing Teams

Few employees, especially in knowledge intensive jobs, operate in isolation any more. Whether a unit designs products or services, delivers them to end users, builds relationships with clients and customers, or provides functional support to the internal operation, work increasingly involves collaboration.

Teams have become a critical leverage point for performance results. Their effectiveness offers an additional source of competitive advantage. Yet most teams are so obsessed with getting things done that they devote no time to the question of how they can be more effective in getting those things done.

Admittedly, teams that ignore their processes and human dynamics still manage to achieve some results. But unresolved conflict, lack of trust, meetings that drone on, inability to make decisions, and lack of accountability and commitment will cripple any group from maximizing its contribution to the enterprise.

Highly productive teams attend to both the tasks they perform and the processes they use. They periodically invest in group time for team building where they can reflect upon the quality of their interpersonal relations and grow their collective capacity to generate even greater results.

A periodic dose of team building improves a group's capacity for results. It fast tracks the development of trust, alignment around goals, identification of the group's operating guidelines, and clarification of individual roles and accountabilities. This is even more true for limited life groups such as project teams and cross-functional/matrix teams.

# What to Do When Your Team Gets "Stuck": 7 Ways to Get It Moving Again

There is no question about it. A team can be a powerful vehicle for accomplishing a major project, guiding a unit to superior performance, or bringing together diverse perspectives to solve a pressing problem

Have you ever been a member of a smooth functioning, high performing team? Those of you who have, no doubt, harbor fond memories of how energizing it is and how great that rush of pride feels when you achieve great things together.

The best teams, including certainly that great team you were on, are not just adept at driving outcomes. They also monitor their process,–how the group deliberates and makes decisions–the morale of the group and the well-being of the individual members. Therefore, the best teams are aware of how well they are doing during a meeting and, when necessary, discuss it openly right on the spot or in a debrief discussion at the end.

## Getting Stuck

Do you remember the last time you were in your car when your wheels were mired deep in a patch of oozy mud (or, for those of you from a colder climate, in a bank of snow and ice)? How heavy it feels to be stuck. How helpless and frustrated you feel. You try to accelerate, spinning your tires faster and faster. If that doesn't work, you try first revving up, then pausing, in an attempt to get a back-and-forth motion going so you can catch the next forward momentum and rocket out of the muck.

While even the best teams get stuck occasionally, most experience this state more often than they realize or admit. I have seen some teams stay stuck for quite awhile, for days, even months.

Just what do I mean by "stuck?" A few examples are when…
• A couple of people continue to dominate the discussion.

- After much debate, you still have two factions pushing their different solutions or goals.
- The discussion goes off agenda and consumes too much time.
- Certain individuals hold up team progress by missing meetings or failing to deliver on task commitments they have made to the group.

The vast majority of teams either are not aware—or simply ignore it—when the team (which is, remember, a group of human beings) becomes stuck. Why? Because "stuckness" is a people issue, a so-called soft skills problem. It calls for courageously confronting the whole group or certain members and potentially with the possibility that strong emotions will be aroused.

## The Cost of Remaining Stuck

You can't afford to deny or ignore it for very long. When your team gets stuck, it can cost you serious money, in at least three ways:

1. The energy and enthusiasm around the table drops off. Team members become discouraged. They start to lose interest in the team's goals. If the situation isn't resolved, their off-line comments about the team turn negative. ("Man, what a waste that meeting was. We're going nowhere. I wish they'd let me drop off this team and just do my regular job.")
2. The extra time each one of you spends spinning team wheels constitutes an opportunity cost. That time and effort could certainly be used more productively elsewhere.
3. Your team may end up squandering the time available for a quality decision on an issue or it may fail to meet promised deadlines. Obviously, poor decisions or missed deliverables can have serious negative repercussions for the operation and for the wider organization.

It pays to recognize when your team is stuck and then intervene quickly to get it humming again. But this still begs two questions: How do you know when your team is, in fact, stuck? What can you do to turn it around?

## Seven Pitfalls and Seven Solutions

Below are seven situations that can cause your team to become bogged down and unproductive. In italics are suggestions of how to respond in order to give your team new found traction.

1. **Lack of Agreement.** We often proceed with the business of the team without everyone being clear and onboard about the team's goals, priorities, tasks and time-lines. Have you ever held a discussion as a group to clarify everybody's expectations regarding objectives, team operating rules and individual roles and accountabilities? *Raise questions when you are not clear about something. Challenge the team to confirm that everyone is on the same page.*

2. **Lack of Commitment.** Sometimes people's initial commitment to the team's goals and agreed-upon priorities wanes. You can hear it in their voices and see it in their record of attendance, participation and delivery on promises made to members. When some people withhold their commitment, it can be a drag on the rest. *Help each member identify benefits that will accrue to him or her personally from the team's success.*

3. **Lack of Accountability.** Are all members following through on tasks they accept responsibility for and promises they make to the group? *Take (your own) accountability for confronting—with respect and for the good of the team—a colleague when he or she does not (take accountability to) deliver on task commitments by the agreed-upon deadline.*

4. **Lack of Leadership.** Whom among you do team members rely upon to step forward and lead? Who keeps the team on target and on agenda? It need not always be the formal leader, the boss. Any member can take the initiative, when needed, to challenge, inspire or confront his/her colleagues. *Ask the manager to be more*

*directive when leading. At the same time, raise the issue with the team that none of you seems to play a leadership role. Or, try stepping in yourself.*

5. **Lack of Communication.** Communication is the lifeblood of your team. It is by communicating that the team makes decisions and gets things done. Are people being authentic when they speak in team discussions? For that matter, is it safe to say what you think, even if it goes against what the group—or the leader—thinks? Does everyone have a chance to contribute? Do members truly dialogue or do they just engage in dueling arguments? *Ask everyone to be more conscious of listening, honoring all points-of-view and disagreeing constructively, with respect.*

6. **Lack of Collaboration.** Some teams, by their very nature, need to collaborate more than others. This is particularly true for groups, such as project teams, that have to share information, reach consensus decisions, and integrate individual tasks into a collective outcome. This, of course, is less of an issue for a management team composed of department heads with little in common other than they report to the same boss. *When collaboration is a must, alert everyone to be sensitive to what their colleagues need and how their own action (or inaction) can impact their team mates' contribution.*

7. **Lack of Trust.** Leadership expert Warren Bennis calls trust the "emotional glue" that holds a team together. It underpins all of the other six elements, above. For trust to be present in your team, members must feel safe to disagree with and confront other individuals or even the team as a whole. They must believe that their colleagues genuinely hold their interests in high regard. *Be patient; trust builds slowly. Encourage everybody to demonstrate their trustworthiness by meeting their commitments and speaking authentically.* In return, others will reciprocate…and trust will grow.

Whether your team is a project, cross-functional, matrix, limited life or a permanent one, it will from time to time become stuck. Look to the above seven factors for the key to pulling your group out of the mud… or the snow!

# Want Greater ROI From Your Meetings? Six Questions That Will Make The Difference

First there's the suffocating volume of e-mails. That is complaint number one. But the next biggest gripe I hear from my clients is that they are spending way too much time in meetings.

Do any of these comments ring true about meetings where you work?
- too long
- no agenda (or, if there is one, we don't follow it)
- rambling, we get off topic a lot
- little is actually decided
- could have just circulated a memo
- the boss does all the talking
- no follow-through on commitments made

I can never quite figure it out? With people so strapped for time, it seems clear that excessive meetings consume a "mother lode" of time that busy people today could put to better use. Why aren't we "mining" time from our meetings.

If you agree with me and want to go after some of that precious time, adopt the following fundamental mind set about your meetings: **treat every meeting as an investment.** Attendees' time and energy are valuable resources. When you call a meeting, always be thinking of how you can maximize the payback on everyone's investment of time.

Here are six questions to ask yourself so your meetings will be productive and satisfying for all involved…and take less time!

## 1. Why am I calling this meeting?
It is an unfortunate fact but the most common reason meetings are convened is to exchange, collect, or pass on information. Be careful. This can be a real waste of time. If more than 25% of your meeting's time is

informational, there is probably a more cost effective way to accomplish this, such as via e-mail or memo.

That said, here are some very good reasons to call a meeting. To…
- ensure that all parties have the same understanding around an issue
- surface new issues
- develop strategies and/or action plans
- address people's reaction to new information, announcements or changes in plans
- solve problems/make decisions
- reconcile differences
- assemble different perspectives and gain commitment

Be crystal clear about your overall purpose before you convene a meeting.

## 2. What specifically do I want to accomplish?
- What are the actual questions or issues to be addressed?
- What are the deliverables or outcomes?
- Will the group actually be making decisions or just providing input?
- Do we want to develop an action plan with time-line commitments around a priority issue or are we simply sharing updates on everybody's activities?

Answers to these questions will determine your agenda, how long your meeting should be, and how much time should be allocated to the various items.

## 3. Whom should I invite?
Consider the opportunity cost for someone attending your meeting vs. the benefit from his or her presence. Remember, when you invite someone you are, in effect, asking the organization to make an investment (of that person's time) in the outcome of your meeting. So. challenge yourself about whose attendance is truly essential and whose is optional?

Furthermore, does everyone need to be there for the entire meeting? Usually not.

Where their attendance does make sense, let your invitees know that it is OK for them to attend only the part where they can add—or receive—value. Further in this spirit, make it absolutely acceptable for invitees to question the need for their presence before they agree to come. In so many organizations, if you decline an invitation, you are seen as devaluing the meeting…and often, by extension, the convener of the meeting.

### 4. What should I do prior to the meeting?

Always send out an agenda, in advance, even if it is just several bullets in a quick e-mail. Solicit any items others would like included in the agenda. To save meeting time, distribute questions, issues, memos, articles, etc., for pre-reading and ask people to come prepared to contribute their ideas or recommendations. Remind specific individuals of any reports or presentations they have committed to make.

### 5. How should I run the meeting?

Start at or within five minutes of the agreed-upon time. Right away this affirms the value of the participants' time and honors those who arrive on time.

It is a fact of organizational life, however, that some people arrive physically in the room at the appointed hour but are not immediately "present." They are preoccupied, mulling over things that have happened earlier or worrying about problems they must deal with after the meeting. One sure sign of this is if their heads are still hunched over their blackberries.

To bring people's conscious attention to this, try opening with something like, "Does anyone need to say or do anything in order to be fully present for this meeting?"

Keep your meeting moving along crisply, according to the agenda. Of course, the discussion may go off track or an item may need more time. If so, stop the conversation and bring this to the group's attention. Obtain people's agreement to deviate from the agenda.

Sometimes the group simply gets stuck, locked in a disagreement or struggling over a definition of terms. How do you recognize when it happens? A good indication—the group's energy drops off. When this happens, interrupt the conversation and describe what you are observing. Say something like:

- "I think we're stuck" or "It feels like we've run out of steam"
- "Does anyone else feel this way?"
- "George and Sally, you've been arguing this same point for the last forty minutes. We need to move on."

### 6. What is the best way to close my meeting?
Always wrap up with these two items:

1. "W3" – who will do what by when? This clarifies decisions made and invites people to take accountability for implementing them.
2. Then, shine the light briefly on "how" your meeting went, with a quick process debrief: "What did we do well today? What, if anything, can we do to be more effective next time?"

If you approach your meetings with these six questions in mind, I promise you, everybody will appreciate it. Your meetings will take less time and your hefty investment in meetings will yield greater returns.

And people who attend will have to find something else to gripe about...once they are exhausted from complaining about those infernal emails.

# What if We Brought in a Facilitator?

Is your upcoming meeting a strategic planning session? A sales or project launch? A departmental communications day? Or, perhaps, team building for an intact management or project team? Whichever it is, it undoubtedly involves a significant investment.

First you have the value of the participants' time, more precious than ever in this time-starved work world. Second, add in the cost of any facility rental, A-V equipment, travel, food and lodging. Finally, and most important, there is the opportunity cost if, following your meeting, plans and decisions are not carried out or your team's behavior does not change for the better.

## When to Use a Facilitator

One way to maximize your investment is to engage the services of a professional facilitator. Of course, not every meeting needs a facilitator but here are four situations where one will pay off for you:

1. *When you want to participate, yourself.* It's not possible to both facilitate and participate. Hey, when they meet even facilitators need a facilitator! Also, a manager cannot effectively facilitate because people will still react to him or her as the boss.
2. *When you will be addressing sensitive issues, including conflict.* An outsider's dispassionate head can diffuse heated exchanges and channel intense emotions into constructive problem-solving.
3. *When your team is stuck.* A skilled facilitator will, with sensitivity, raise to the group issues that are being avoided or even dysfunctional behaviors that are being denied. In so doing, he/she can help the team move to a new level of productive functioning.
4. *When your group will be dealing with complex issues and a variety of viewpoints.* A seasoned facilitator brings to your meeting a wealth of group processes and activities to scope issues, generate options, make decisions and build consensus.

# What a Facilitator Does

In a nutshell, they design and manage your meeting's process, ensure you achieve the meeting's objectives, and help your group or team learn and enhance its ongoing effectiveness beyond the meeting.

*Prior to your session* he/she will help you clarify your desired meeting outcomes and design an agenda and process to meet those goals. In some cases, depending upon the issues, your facilitator may recommend some up front diagnostic work. For example, he/she might send out a survey questionnaire or even conduct one-on-one interviews, by phone or in person, with a cross-section or all of the participants. The purpose here would be to collect different perspectives on specific issues or generate advance input to work with at the meeting.

*During the meeting*, let your facilitator lead the process, so you can become as actively involved as possible as a participant. He/she will keep the meeting moving forward, respond appropriately to significant, unforeseen issues that arise, and move the group to closure at the end, accomplishing the objectives for which you have contracted. Normally you will need check in only occasionally with him/her regarding the meeting's direction and progress.

*The post-meeting* period is when your group puts into action what was agreed upon in the session. Your facilitator can suggest ways to keep the meeting's decisions and commitments alive in the weeks and months that follow. This could involve the facilitator's following-up with individuals, a brief survey of progress to-date and results achieved, or even a group "booster" meeting for participants to report in and maintain the momentum.

# What to Look for in Your Facilitator

Facilitation is different from public speaking and training. It is not about having solid content, good platform skills and an understanding of adult learning principles. Facilitation is about working with groups of people in the moment. That is, being tuned in at all times to what is happening and being able to suspend or change the process accordingly.

Here are five attributes to look for when selecting a professional to guide your session:

1. *Superb communications skills.* Especially the ability to listen intently and to come up with the right words and tone to address a tense situation.
2. *Comfortable "in their own shoes."* The self-confidence to be on the receiving end of confrontational words and either stand their ground or admit their error.
3. *Willingness to put the group first.* When facilitating, the group is the "star," not the facilitator. Big egos do not make good facilitators.
4. *Understanding of group process theory.* He/she should be able to apply concepts such as leadership, group norms, stages of team development, systems theory, dialogue and experiential learning to the design and facilitation of your meeting.
5. *Flexibility to let the process unfold.* While advance planning is important for your meeting's success, things come up in the session itself that require, for the good of the group, that you alter the plan-perhaps even throw it out completely. A rigid, control-oriented facilitator can frustrate your group and torpedo your results.

## Results You Can Expect

If you use a facilitator in any of the four conditions that call for one, you are almost certain to accomplish more in your session, delve deeper into critical issues and resolve them, and have your participants leave with positive feelings, cohesiveness, a sense of accomplishment, and a renewed belief in the team.

Now that constitutes a solid payback on your investment!

# Kickstarting a Brand New Team

Do you remember the last time you attended the initial meeting of a new task force or project team at work? No one could agree on the goals. A couple of people complained about all their other work demands. Someone was pushing a personal agenda to become the team "leader." After a couple of hours of struggle, with the "team's" wheels totally spinning, you began to ask yourself why you were here.

In high performance organizations with project-oriented environments, ad hoc teams are becoming the norm. Examples are companies like Levi Strauss, ABB, and 3M.

Temporary teams differ from permanent teams. Most importantly, they have *high demands placed on them to produce results quickly and then disband.* Their mandate and authority (e.g. can they make final decisions? can they implement them?) are often unclear. And if the team is also cross-functional, it will have complex goals affecting many parts of the organization and beyond.

And then there are the team members! They come with varying degrees of commitment, different agenda, functional backgrounds, perspectives, and loyalties. But they all wonder whether their efforts here will be rewarded at performance review time.

*The ad hoc team faces a unique challenge.* It must sort out its human dynamics issues early, get everyone aligned on a common mandate, and build the genuine commitment of all members to that goal quickly! These teams seldom have enough time to devote to the project. They need to get on with the task—asap! Yet, again and again experience has shown that *when team members do not address the human dynamics part right at the beginning, team performance suffers seriously later on.*

So, what should your project or ad hoc team do to maximize its performance? Its first meeting is crucial. Plan to invest just one day, up front, on its "process" issues. This initial session should be facilitated by a skilled person who is not a team member. As a guide, here is what my one-day "kickstart" program typically covers:

## Purpose/mission

Why was the team created? What goals and deliverables (e.g. design a process to reduce wastage by 18%) are expected of it? Ensure that all members understand and accept these objectives and their related time-lines.

## Champion(s)

To which manager, board member, or steering committee does the team report? What support has this champion promised? What information/ updates do they expect from the team? How will the team liaise with the champion?

## Team Members

What skills, knowledge, and experience do they bring? Identify and discuss each person's hopes, desired benefits, expectations, concerns, and initial degree of commitment to the team. Make it OK not to be committed at the outset.

## Operating Guidelines

Determine how leadership will operate within the team. Is there one leader? What is his/her role? How will the team make decisions? How often will they meet? How will they communicate amongst one another? What is expected of each member? Can someone miss a meeting? What happens if someone fails to meet a commitment?

## Next Steps (the team will take)

Now it is time to turn the group onto its task. Here members start developing a plan of action and assign responsibilities. The day should end with this underway.

The above fills a very productive day first day of team operation, so here it pays to engage a facilitator to fast track your team to performance. The facilitator will:

1. Provide structure and leadership
2. Train members on what they need to know about group dynamics
3. Help team members get through the initial energy-draining issues around power
4. Ensure that your team members stay focused

A good facilitator will leave the team with tools and techniques to address interpersonal issues whenever they obstruct team performance downline.

What about your temporary teams? Do they have enough time for a slow acceleration to maximum performance? Can they afford it?

# Your Group Doesn't Have to Be a "Team"

One of the best books written on teams and teamwork is *The Wisdom of Teams* by Jon Katzenbach and Douglas Smith. They make the distinction between a "team" and what they call a "working group."

The latter is the most common form in workplaces today. For example:
- a VP with a group of managers, each in charge of a functional area of the department
- an accounting manager with a group of employees spread over the various jobs within the department.

In most cases, all you need is a working group. These are absolutely appropriate where the work products of the group members are primarily individual, where the group's overall output is essentially the sum of the individual inputs, and where rewards are based on individual, rather than group, performance.

To turn a "working group" into a "team" (and especially the "high performing" variety) requires a significant investment of team time to develop its processes, identify and commit to genuinely shared goals, build major levels of trust, openness and mutual accountability, and learn–often painfully–how to share direct, pointed and sensitive feedback within the group.

You would choose to make such an investment only if what you expect from the group is a **collective** performance output, where the very nature of the work requires members to collaborate, and where individual actions and decisions will positively or negatively affect overall performance. Many project teams fall into this category.

Now, I'm a big fan of team building retreats and the like. I facilitate them as part of my professional work. And make no mistake about it, where appropriate, creating a true team will payoff big in performance results. But too often we try to push groups to become teams when they don't need to be. So, before you rush off and do team building with your group, clarify why you are doing this and what outcomes you want to achieve. Talk it over with the facilitator. Don't pay for more than you need.

# Allow Team Members to Find Their Place

Edgar Schein, a titan of the field of organizational development, says in his recent book, *Helping*, that there are **four questions on the minds of new members of any team.** While these concerns operate at a subconscious level, nevertheless, any team member must become comfortable with the answers before he or she can relax and start to really contribute to team goals. These personal issues are:

- What role am I to play in this group? In effect, who am I to be?
- How much control or influence will I have with these people?
- Will being part of the team meet my own goals and needs?
- How personally close and sharing are we expected to be?

Members work out at least some initial answers during the very first stage of team development, the so-called "forming" stage, where people start to get to know the other members and test out where they stand, to what degree they will be accepted into the team, where they fit in the group's power structure (sometimes called the "pecking order"), and whether or not this will be a positive experience.

The wise leader understands this reality and does all she can to enable team members to get these questions answered for themselves so they can quickly proceed to establish the solid foundation of trust which team high performance always requires.

This is why when I facilitate a team building process I always allocate significant time for the team to collaborate on their goals & priorities, core values, and how they agree to work together. I show them how to use the *Teamwork Palette* (http://www.888fulcrum.com/teamwork-palette/) tool to foster conversations and decisions that reflect a consensus about how they will "be" as a team. While this is going on, individual members begin to discover their own place–how they will "be"–in the group.

The result: they find acceptable answers for themselves to Edgar Schein's four questions.

# Team Process Makes All the Difference

All teams must pay attention to their work: the task, the goal, the things to be done, the agenda items to be crammed into their meetings, the hurried decisions to be made by the group, the deadlines to be met, and so on.

But **the most effective teams** also monitor how well the members are working together and what the current "climate" is within the team. They quickly notice when the team becomes stuck or bogged down or loses energy and enthusiasm. When this occurs, team members stop working the task they are on and turn their attention to the team's stalled process.

Successful teams have learned that the sooner they sort out any human dynamics that are getting in the way of doing the job well, the sooner the team can get on with the work to be done.

Most teams these days are so totally task-oriented and deadline-driven that they either ignore or don't notice dysfunction when it emerges in their midst. People just plow on, trying to get the job done while becoming more and more frustrated and less and less enthusiastic about their involvement in the group.

So, try to make it your team's standard operating procedure to take regular readings of the climate in your group. This is particularly important during the early period of your team's existence. However, occasional readings should also be carried out later on, even once your team seems to be running well.

We have a powerful team tool to help you do this, called the *Teamwork Palette*®. I invite you to check it out. (http://www.888fulcrum.com/teamwork-palette/)

# Trust the Process

Years ago when I was taking courses from *University Associates* around how to facilitate groups, a wise instructor named Larry Porter said these three words: *Trust the process.* I have never forgotten them. They have been my anchor at critical times when, facilitating a team building session, I find the conversation seems about to get out of hand. This raises the level of anxiety within the team and also in the facilitator.

The "worst case" fear (and isn't that the one that we always bring to the fore whenever we worry?), of course, is that harsh words will be said, relationships will be damaged, and the team will suffer irreparable harm. What Larry taught me was to guard against acting too quickly, simply to reduce my own anxiety.

He said that groups are endowed with a built-in gyroscope. They have a remarkable capacity to self-regulate when things become too hot. Groups possess an innate sense of how much conflict the group can handle and they pull back when that limit is reached. I have seen this again and again over the years as groups have regularly surprised me (and frequently themselves, for that matter). They are almost always more capable to grow and stretch in terms of human dynamics than they appear to be.

This doesn't mean that it's OK for the facilitator to sit off to the side and watch the team implode. You do have to listen to your experience and intuition as to when to intervene, if necessary.

Whether you are a team leader or a facilitator, when the group starts to rise to a new level of openness and candidness, by all means be vigilant but also be willing to sit with your anxiety. Allow your group's to gyro kick in and watch the team shift to a higher degrees of performance potential.

Remember, it's about building the team's capacity, not maintaining your personal comfort level.

# Don't Neglect Team Maintenance

You plan to drive your car from Boston to Denver. It's a long trip so, before departing, you take your vehicle into your local service center for a tune-up. You have them check your tires and battery, top up the oil and brake fluid and take it for a spin on the highway listening for any rattles that should not be rattling.

Then, once on your journey when you stop for gas, even if everything seems fine, you do a quick check on how your vehicle is operating. If you don't perform these maintenance checks, your car may overheat, stall or completely break down somewhere out there on the great plains. At best, you will be delayed. At the worst, you never make it to your destination.

Your team is like your automobile. Instead of taking you from "Beantown" to the "Mile High City," however, your team is designed to do something else: make decisions, perform tasks, achieve a specific goal. But, just like your car, your team needs maintenance checks, both at the outset and along the way. Otherwise, the team risks becoming stuck, limping along, under performing, and even breaking down completely. The result: it fails to accomplish its goals.

Our teams and departmental work groups seldom reach their true potential. If only more of them had the wisdom (and the guts, let's be honest) to attend to the maintenance of the group, especially when its ability to solve problems, make decisions and produce results hits an obstacle or gradually degrades. They would remove the obstacle, reverse the decline, and head directly toward a highly desirable destination… called *high performance.*

# Communicating Effectively... In Every Direction

To flourish in today's environment enterprises must respond with:

- fast-paced decisions made at the front-line
- virtual teams spread across distant work locations
- work based increasingly on knowledge and creativity
- solutions that require collaboration to bring into being
- agile responses to the rapidly shifting demands of markets
- informal networking within and beyond the organization
- culturally diverse workforces
- flat organization designs where the individual manager is responsible for a greater number of direct reports

Because of this, communication has become ever more essential for high quality results, satisfied customers, and a profitable operation. It underpins the effectiveness of everything that leaders, teams and individual contributors do.

Savvy enterprises insist that their team and leader development strategies include both the skills and the core attitudes that underlie excellent interpersonal communication. They know that it is the only way they can survive in this challenging marketplace.

# Trust, Communications, Leadership...and Retention

I was approached recently by a prospective client who wants a workshop as part of an internal strategic initiative around communications between the levels. They want to focus on:
- 2-way communication, down to the employee and upward to the manager
- what should be communicated and when
- obstacles to communicating more openly
- how to solicit communication from staff
- listening
- creating a climate where it's safe to speak your mind

This stuff just doesn't go away as an issue, does it? I heard similar concerns when I started my training and consulting practice 22 years ago.

Nevertheless, my potential client is wise to address these concerns. Why? Look no further than Deloitte's 2010 *Ethics and Workplace Survey*.

Here are just a few things they discovered from their research:
- 1/3 of employed Americans planned to look for a new job when the economy is more stable.
- 48% of these with an eye on greener employment pastures cited "loss of trust" as a major contributing factor to their intention to look elsewhere.
- 46% of them mentioned "lack of transparency in communications."
- 40% included "being treated unfairly or unethically by employers."

Now, here's the question that should concern my prospect and all of us. Is this 1/3 block of employees made up mostly of the best employees, the ones you really don't want to lose, the ones who will cost you a ton to replace?

My guess is yes.

# Communicating Your Core Brand Message – Internally!

Not long ago I attended a presentation by Mark Carrier, Senior Vice President of the Hotel Division of the B.F. Saul Company. This company has won a number of awards around excellence in innovation, HR leadership, and Marriott's Spirit to Preserve award. They manage 18 hotels of well-known brands, primarily in the Washington, DC area.

Carrier's talk was about how they instilled in every employee's mind and in every corner of their operations their core values that inform how the company operates, what they call, with great fanfare, "Our Big Three":

1. Happy, professional team members who demonstrate aggressive friendliness.
2. A clean, crisp, safe property where everything works.
3. Guests and team members receive all that they expect…plus a little bit more.

What they have done is apply the principles of traditional branding *within* the organization. With the aid of a recognizable logo and a variety of strategies, they have been working for five years to gradually have all of their employees living the brand experience.

Here are a few of the many ways they do this:
- Their company mascot, "OB3," appears at company gatherings, from shareholder meetings to employee parties.
- Each new manager receives a high quality pen with logo and is asked to use it whenever signing their name in the course of their work.
- Every new employee receives a pocket size laminated card with ten guidelines to work behavior that reflect the "Our Big 3" values. For example: know your hotel, present a polished image, details make the difference, create a "wow."
- The performance review document (which by the way, they call the "Big 3 Report Card,") groups performance items under the Our Big 3 categories.

On face it struck me as a bit hokey and over the top but, when you think about it, good marketing involves repeated messaging in a number of delivery formats. Besides, wouldn't you be inclined to come back to a hotel where you experience aggressive friendliness, a clean/crisp/safe facility, and a bit more than you expect? I would.

# What to Do about Those Infernal Grousers

At the opening of a four-day management training program I delivered I asked the participants what learnings they wanted to take away from the program. Spread across the lists they shared were a number of versions of "how to deal with negativity in the workplace."

I wasn't surprised, as I encounter this as an issue for most managers. At the same time, a part of me was disappointed. How sad that so many managers out there encounter a negative outlook in the heads of their employees. Now, dear reader, we can commiserate about this fact and acknowledge that the sources of this negativity are many and complex.

Better, however, for us to direct our attention onto what a manager can do about it. So, here's what I told the participants in my program.

## Chronically negative people are blamers.

- They are continually filtering for *what's wrong* and, at the drop of a hat, will let you know who is to blame for the problem. (By the way, have you noticed how it the blamer is never at fault? Blamers would never say, "The problem around here is nobody communicates and, in fact, I am one of the worst offenders.")
- They don't really want solutions to their complaints. That will just jeopardize the (comfortable, thank you very much) problem-centered lens through which they view their employer organization.
- Life is simple when it's not their fault. Add to this that wonderful feeling of being "right" and even a tad superior to those who are running the place.
- These people let their "victim child" side of their personality run rampant. They refuse to allow their "adult" side to join the discussion and offer how they might, in fact, be contributing to the predicament and what responsibility they accept for working toward a solution.

# Gently, with respect, throw a spanner into their thinking process.

- The next time your frequent complainer expresses a negative, unfocused criticism, respond with something like:
  - » "How would you like things to be instead?"
  - » "What would it look like if this problem were fixed?"
  - » "What's missing for you that, if present, would make this not a problem anymore?"
- When an employee complains to you about another employee, respond with:
  - » "What would you prefer that they do instead?"
  - » "Are they aware of what they are doing?"
  - » "Furthermore, do they realize how much it is bugging you?"
  - » "Have you told them what you want from them?"

# Be persistent and unwavering with these responses and before you know it the grouser will stop being negative, at least with you.

By using approaches like these, you invite them to shift their focus from the problem itself to possible solutions for the problem. You are asking them to take *accountability* for getting their needs met. After all, that's what adults do.

# Dealing with Resistance: the 4 + 2 Method

We've all lived this before. Sally, the manager, asks her employee Gary to prepare a market analysis report for next week. Gary moans and says he doesn't think he can do it by then . . . too much work and, besides, why not give it to Sherry who has a marketing background. The manager detects the "I don't wanna" whine and feels the heavy inertia of Gary's heels digging in.

At that moment what Sally really wants to do is to respond in the old style of leadership, with both barrels blazing: "I don't want any excuses, Gary, just see that YOU have that on my desk by Tuesday!" or the much more subtle "There you go again, Gary. Don't you think it's about time you showed some initiative around here?"

In fact, this exemplifies a common, yet absolutely critical, point of choice for any manager. Will Sally or will she not choose to assume responsibility for making Gary change his behavior and attitude? She assumes responsibility whenever she decides to challenge the resistance by overpowering it or manipulating Gary with guilt or threats.

Tempting as it might be, this approach does not really accomplish what Sally, the leader, wants. It might generate Gary's short-term compliance but what she sacrifices is his longer-term commitment, creativity and productivity. By trying to make the resister do her bidding she shifts herself into the parent position and maneuvers him or her into the role of the child.

In Gestalt psychology this situation is called the **"Top Dog/Under Dog"** dynamic. The *Top Dog* is the boss, the master, the authority figure, the one who seeks a certain behavior from the other person. The *Under Dog* is—ostensibly—the powerless one, the slave, the victim and the one from whom the behavior is being demanded. But who has the real power in the long run? The Under Dog does. It is he/she who ultimately determines whether or not cooperation will be forthcoming.

So, if browbeating a resister just heightens the resistant force, what's a leader to do? The answer lies in understanding what the Under Dog truly wants. The resisting Under Dog primarily wants to be acknowledged, to be heard, to have his or her point-of-view honored—not necessarily agreed with.

This last point is critical for leaders to grasp. When someone resists your will no one expects you to just cave in and abdicate your responsibility for performance results. At the same time, if you can make the resister feel heard and truly understood by you, he/she will be more inclined to consider your position and buy into it. Remember, one of Stephen Covey's famous "7 Habits" is "Seek first to understand and then be understood."

Here is a "cutting edge" approach that draws from both Gestalt psychology and the martial art of Aikido. I call this the 4 + 2 Method. There are six steps: the first four focus you on the other person. With the last two you assert your own needs.

- Consciously acknowledge to yourself that you are encountering resistance.
- *Center yourself.* (Use deep breathing or even a brief meditation, if you have time.)
- In your own mind, consciously grant them permission to take the position they are adopting.
- *Explore, investigate, become curious about their resistance.* (Use questions to find out about the source of their opposition.)
- Declare your own perceptions, expectations, requirements and rationale.
- *Resolve/decide/act as you see fit.* (Here you exercise your ultimate responsibility for performance results.)

Try it out on the next time you encounter a low-risk situation of resistance. Notice the response of the resister and how your own stress is reduced. With practice you will be surprised at how often you turn resistance into genuine support.

# Are You a "Director" or an "Informer?"

Here's an easy way to look at how you communicate **when you want to influence someone to do something**. It is a simple, practical model that comes from Interstrength Associates.

Imagine line running from *Directing* at one end to *Informing* at the other.

**Directing** communication comes across as a clearly stated request or demand. There is no doubt that you want someone to do something. At the extreme is sounds like an order: "Bring me your report." In a softer form (more toward the center of the line) it come out like: "Your report was due last Friday so would you please get it to me today."

**Informing** communication sounds much more tentative. It *implies a request* by providing information (hence, informing) but does not make the request outright. At the far Informing end of that line you might hear: "I still haven't seen your report." Moving along the line you get something like: "I need to see your report and was wondering if it's ready yet."

That line between Directing and Informing is, in fact, a continuum and we all have a place of comfort along it when we express our needs for others to do something.

There are times, of course when speaking from either extremity of the continuum is appropriate and not disconcerting to those who receive your message. For example:

- You choose very **Directing** language because of a time pressure and you need someone to focus laser-like on the task at-hand.
- Purely **Informing** language works well when you want to motivate people to make an independent choice to do an action or when you want to enroll them in a wider process.


But a problem can arise when a manager needs to get greater buy-in and participation from his or her people but is naturally directive in his/her speech. This element of a boss's communication style can be changed with feedback and coaching. I find the opposite problem if more often the case, however—managers who want to come across more assertively but continue to use an extremely informative style. The good news is that, if a non-assertive manager *consciously* adopts a more directive delivery, over time he/she will become comfortable with how that sounds and will incorporate it into his/her default speaking style.

Words do make a difference. Does what you say when influencing your staff project the "you" you want them to experience?

# We Listen but Do We Really Care?

They say we all should cultivate the ability to listen. "Why?" we ask. They say it shows respect, it makes the other person feel included, it honors the other's point-of-view, it reduces tension, it takes the energy out of opposition.

But seldom do they tell us that it is the best way for us to learn. Seldom do they mention that, through listening and understanding, we and the other person can search together for the fullest truth or the best solution…that neither of us usually has.

Dan Balz and Haynes Johnson, in their book, *The Battle for America 2008: The Story of an Extraordinary Election,* quote Barack Obama explaining why he so admires Abraham Lincoln.

> *…there is just a deep-rooted honesty and empathy to the man that allowed him to always be able to see the other person's point of view and always sought to find that truth that is in the gap between you and me. Right? That the truth is out there somewhere and I don't fully possess it and you don't fully possess it and our job then is to listen and learn and imagine enough to be able to get to that truth.*

This ability to listen in dialogue with another, where you are willing to suspend your own truths in order to learn from the other's truths and perhaps be swayed by them, is a major milepost on the road to advanced development as a human being, let alone as an excellent manager.

It is so easy to **pretend**–to ourself and to our employees–that we are listening and that we care. But when we show up in a conversation able to truly take in what they are saying, our level of trustworthiness in the mind of the employee shoots up dramatically.

Of course, know that you aren't quite there yet if you have to grit your teeth and furrow your forehead as you try hard to listen.

# Mirror, Mirror, in Our Brains

I know you have had an experience similar to this.

During a recent planning meeting of a volunteer group the conversation was flowing, people were at ease, light hearted opening pleasantries had been shared and we were tackling the first agenda item in a positive, upbeat spirit. Ten minutes into the discussion a key member showed up. He was uncharacteristically subdued and did not respond to our welcomes in his usually smiling way.

The mood in the team shifted palpably, in a heartbeat. I know I felt a heaviness in my stomach area. We continued on, with his involvement, but it never felt the same. We became more businesslike, humor faded from the conversation, and I found myself making as little eye contact as possible with the late comer.

What this incident demonstrated is the power of what neuroscientists are calling *mirror neurons*. These are neurons that fire both when we
1.  feel and express an emotion and
2.  sense a similar emotional state in another person.


PBS' NOVA ScienceNOW has a great little video on mirror neurons. (http://www.pbs.org/wgbh/nova/body/mirror-neurons.html)

In situation #1, if I am both feeling angry and expressing it in my face, body posture, gestures, voice tone, etc., certain neurons relating to my emotional state will be firing. That's pretty straight forward. But, in situation #2, if I sense anger in you—by my observing your non-verbal cues—those same anger-related neurons that fired independently in me in situation #1 will fire once again *in my brain*. They are, in effect, "mirroring" your emotional state in my brain and I will most likely experience the very same emotion you are feeling.

But what does the discovery of mirror neurons have to do with being a "best boss?"

Here are three points I invite you to consider:

1. As a manager, the impact of having your current mood permeate the minds of your employees is much greater simply because you are the boss! If one employee down at the end of the table is in a funk, the group can, if it chooses, get on quite well anyway. If it's the boss who is in the funk, however, it's really hard for staff to ignore it and keep up and positive despite it.

2. If you find yourself in a negative mood, consciously intervene to either change your mood or mask it when interacting with others. Best bosses cannot afford the luxury of letting a foul mood go unchecked at work.

3. The flip of this: realize that your positive, upbeat, confident state-of-mind will contaminate (a good thing here) the moods of your staff, peers and customers. Cultivate these elements in yourself and you will energize your people to perform at remarkably higher levels and do so consistently.

Part of being a good leader is being a good actor.

# It's Scary How Easily We Slip into Judging Mode

A number of years ago my wife and I attended a workshop on how to facilitate dialogue. The session was led by our colleagues Will Stockton and Marjorie Herdes of Mobius, Inc. (http://www.mobiusmodel.com) They do tremendous work, especially facilitating large group and community dialogue sessions, using a "roadmap" they've evolved over the years which they call the Mobius Model.

In the course of our workshop they facilitated a dialogue between us around something that had happened awhile back about which we had different views. It wasn't a huge issue between us but, experiencing my end of the dialogue with my wife, I stumbled upon a huge insight.

It is so very easy to stop listening to the other person and, **while they are still talking**, shift over to making judgment calls about what they are saying. I fancied myself as an expert in interpersonal communications, so I was doubly infuriated to see myself doing this. She would make a point and, in the privacy of my mind I would begin a silent monologue about how...

- she had that point wrong
- her recollection was clearly faulty here
- there is a good reason why I said what I did (in the situation under discussion)
- I will respond just as soon as she stops talking

True, clear, open communication is easy—in theory. Daily we fool ourselves that we are being attentive and focused on the essence of what the other person is saying. It's not true. We rarely focus for more than a few precious seconds—just long enough for them to get out a complete thought, so we can begin crafting an "editorial" about it in our mind.

Don't believe me? Start observing your internal dialogue in your next few interactions, Yeah, do it with the next person that walks in the door.

# Individual Development

It goes without saying that organizations play a leading role in developing the capacity of their employees. Enterprises invest in their staff in order to raise the level of their contribution closer to their full potential. More often than not it is the employer that takes the initiative and drives this process.

Yet who, in fact, lies at the center of the development process? The individual employee, the person who must actually do the growing. If he (she) is to build his job and career capacity, he must make some choices:

- Does he want to learn and grow?
- If so, in what areas?
- How badly does he want it?
- How hard is he willing to work to make it happen?
- Is he open to feedback and to new ideas about how best to operate?

The manager would do well to understand this reality: if any learning is to take place, it will be ultimately up to the employee.

A boss should challenge her employees, periodically bringing up the existential questions about how happy they currently are in their job and what more they want—beyond money—at this point in their career. The responses to queries such as these will tell the company whether investment in a particular employee's development will land on fertile or fallow ground.

# Keep (Career) Development on the Table

In the hurly burly of meeting deadlines, doing more with less, and achieving performance goals, it is easy to forget to keep up the dialogue with each of your staff about:

1. How they are doing vis-à-vis their performance
2. How they are doing vis-à-vis their well-being
3. Their continuing development and growth

And, if we do manage to carve out the time to talk about any of the above, it's usually about performance. Heck, we can leave the "softer stuff" for year-end performance review discussion, no?

Well, according to a Right Management study, too many managers–37%, in fact–**never** get around to talking about #3.

It's a shame that employees' individual development is off the radar screen of so many managers because, let's face it, their own development is obviously a top concern for most employees. Furthermore, managers caring–genuinely–about their employees' well being and development consistently shows up in studies as a major driver of employee engagement.

Just because times are hard and the jobs aren't out there at the moment, career development still matters to your staff (and to you too, I betcha). Stephen Covey famously called it "sharpening the saw." If you stop investing in staff development, those saws will gradually become dull.

So, think of each of your employees, individually. When was the last time you broached the subject of the on-going development of his/her capacity? If you can't remember, don't wait. Have that conversation right away.

# Do We Stop Growing after Schooling?

I ran across a recent posting from the *Gallup Management Journal* that made a point have I never thought about before:

> *"Raised through a childhood in which each new year brought novel opportunities, playing at ever more difficult levels of sports, growing physically, educated in a system of cleanly delineated grades -- freshman, sophomore, junior, senior -- many employees find themselves several years into their career wondering what happened to the momentum they used to enjoy. Being both conditioned and naturally wired to look forward to differences between seventh and eighth grade or high school and college, many workers are disappointed to discover there will be no dramatic difference between their experience as a 25-year-old employee and their experience as a 26-year-old employee."*

The full article talks about the plethora of studies that show what a powerful motivator is personal and professional growth, learning, and rising to a tough-but-attainable challenge.

So many people, in their jobs, no longer feel any sense of increasing their capacity and moving on to more challenging tasks. Each day is the same, each year essentially a clone of the last one. Clearly, one cause of this is structural. Some jobs, especially in manufacturing and straight forward service functions, are repetitive and have had any meaningful discretion engineered out of them.

But, in the vast number of jobs, this is not the case. Here it is incumbent upon managers to periodically ask what their employees have learned and how they have grown over the last year. Better still, however, let's get out in front of the curve. At least once a year—perhaps at performance review time—ask each of your staff members,

"What do would like to learn/know/be able to do 12 months from today that you don't know or can't do today?"

I believe the best bosses are catalysts for the never-ending growth of every employee in their charge.

# Toxic Mix = Bully Boss

Certain chemicals are inert and harmless standing alone but, when combined, they combust into toxic fumes, or worse. This, apparently, is what frequently happens when a boss becomes a bully.

A series of studies reported last year in the academic journal, Psychological Science, (http://www.ncbi.nlm.nih.gov/pubmed/19818043) found that bosses who abuse employees tend to be the result of two factors:
1. Being in a position of power over others
2. Feelings of incompetence and self-doubts of their ability


It takes both of these to produce a true bully in the manager's chair. This goes deep, psychologically. The abusive boss's ego may be threatened, not necessarily from more competent employees but often from deep-seated feelings of inadequacy.

I'm hearing more references to bullying in management than I used to. In fact, a colleague of mine, Valerie Cade, specializes in this issue (http://www.performancecurve.com). I don't think it has necessarily grown but we seem to be more sensitive to its presence. One study indicated that in the U.S. thirty seven per cent of employees claim to have been been abused by their boss. This includes being yelled at, dressed down in the presence of peers or given the silent treatment.

What can you do if you report to a tyrant? The same study found that one proven strategy, at least for the short run, is to flatter your boss and affirm his (or her) strengths. They found, however, that there was a downside to this approach—it can reinforce the boss's delusion of competence and distance him/her further from the painful truth. Besides, that strategy feels phony. Your flattery will probably be false.

Here two suggestions if you are faced with a toxic manager. First of all, **be extremely careful!** You may well be dealing with pathological behavior on his part. Secondly, if you can't engage him in an adult-to-adult conversation about how you are experiencing him and the impact it is having on you, accept that you are not in a position to get him to change. It's beyond your influence. Go over his head to his boss or to a neutral party, such as your HR department.

You will be doing your organization—and your boss—a huge favor.

# Raise Your Gaze:
# Staying Energized in the Daily Grind

It is mid afternoon. You are sitting at your desk trying to pull together this important proposal for your boss. It is due the day after tomorrow. As you wrestle with how to incorporate a complex spreadsheet from the finance department, you wonder when your quality analyst will bring in those last two key pieces of production information. Then there is still your own summary piece to write. But what will you write? The recommendations just aren't coming from your brain.

We have all been there. You hit a point when it feels like you are trudging through quicksand. Everything is difficult. Your energy and enthusiasm for the task is dropping rapidly. It's no longer any fun. You begin to question your own ability to do this work. You just want it off your plate—done!

How do we typically respond in a situation like this? When we finally stop procrastinating, we typically just grit our teeth, hunker down and try harder to focus on the detailed steps and problems, one-by-painful-one. All the while we talk to ourselves, allowing our silent critic to castigate us for our incompetence or beseeching our-reluctant-cheerleader self to give us a pep talk . . ."Go get 'em. You can do this. No sweat, piece of cake." Instead of focusing on our work, our thoughts dwell on ourselves and how we are (not) performing.

Of course, this is not a productive state-of-mind to be in. In fact, it is the polar opposite of what researcher Michael Csikzentmihalyi calls the "flow" state. Flow is an optimal performance mental mode where you forget about yourself and merge with your activity. You feel challenged yet in control. It is a timeless state-you don't notice the clock. People often experience it in sports, at play or when truly engaged by work. Above all, flow is a productive place to be.

There is a way to climb out when you are mired in a " mental valley." Try it out yourself and coach your employees to do the same.

You must get in touch with two images.

First, consciously remind yourself what the goal of your activity is and picture how you will feel when it is done. In the opening scenario, your goal is the finished report. You could decide to replace your self-defeating, negative thoughts with images of handing it over to your boss and how great and proud you feel doing it.

Secondly, remind yourself why you are in this line of work in the first place. This gets you back in touch with your overall purpose and with the real meaning behind your efforts. Again, in the opening scenario, you would tell yourself why this report is important, how it will contribute to the organization and whom specifically it will positively affect.

When you raise your gaze above the sometimes draining details of your job, you rekindle your energy and begin feeling creative, confident and motivated. Best of all, you will get the job done and achieve the results you are seeking.

WOULD THEY CALL YOU THEIR BEST BOSS EVER?

# What's Your Current Edge for Development?

They have a momentary pause of puzzlement when I ask them. So, I put the question to my audience again,

> *"What is your current edge for development?"*

"What do you mean?" they ask. "I mean," I say, "if you could snap your fingers and instantly improve significantly in one aspect of your work that would have the greatest leverage on your overall effectiveness, what would it be?" "Oh" say their faces as they proceed to ponder the query.

For many people this is a difficult question. For some, absolutely nothing comes to mind! Managers in my sessions have a variety of responses…
- think more strategically—vs. responding to "crises" all the time
- be able to confront a poor performer without my own legs turning to jelly
- lead meetings that are satisfying and accomplish a great deal
- organize my desk and deploy myself according to my priorities.

Try out the question right now. Come on now,

> *What is your current edge for development?*

This is a vitally important question for each of us to ask ourselves regularly. It is the driver that keeps us continually learning. And when you come up with your answer, I have a follow-up question for you,

> *"What do you intend to do over the next twelve months to develop this ability?"*

As a professional speaker, my current edge is to build more stories into my presentations. I've avoided them because, I imagine, it will be difficult. I don't notice stories. I don't remember stories. I don't even like stories in other people's presentations. Yet I know they will add more to the overall impact of my message than anything else I could present.

How can you identify your current edge? Ask people—your boss, your peers, your staff, your customers…your significant other! Consult your last performance review. Or, consider your vision for yourself in, say, two years' time. What knowledge, skills, and/or attitudes are missing that would make that vision a reality?

Then, develop and implement a plan to acquire these attributes. When you have succeeded, return to the question. A new edge for development will emerge, returning you to being a (beginner) learner. This is what "continual learning" means. And I believe it is the only way we can survive in this crazy, convulsive world.

Managers, professionals, and knowledge workers must master a complex weave of competencies. Author George Leonard calls mastery, "the mysterious process during which what is at first difficult becomes progressively easier and more pleasurable through practice." Notice that mastery is a process, not a destination. We must never cease.

Jigoro Kano, the founder of judo, was a consummate "master." But when he died he asked to be buried with a white belt on.

# Cultural Neuroscience –
# The Brain in Action Again

Not surprisingly, although I had never heard about it before, there is a branch of brain research that studies:

1. How cultural traits to which we are exposed impact our brains
2. How our brain and its processes impact the emergence and transmission of cultural traits

*Newsweek* (Oct. 17, 2010) had an interesting short article by Sharon Begley that offers just a glimpse into this field. She recounts a study comparing how, for Chinese and Westerners, the medial prefrontal cortex (a section of the brain) swung into action when they pondered whether a particular adjective describes themselves. The same area activated for both groups.

What is interesting is that the *same brain area* also fired for the Chinese when considering whether the word applied as well to their mother. For the Westerners, it did not. For them, there was no overlap.

What can we in management do with this information? I'm not sure. But for me it just underlines how powerfully our culture, experiences and thoughts carve deep neural pathways in our brain circuitry, pathways that guide our default, unconscious behavior and decisions. Begley puts it so much better:

…our lives leave footprints on the bumps and fissures of our cortex.

# Up Your Self-Awareness to the Next Level

I am a fan of the theory and research linking one's level of adult development to one's effectiveness as a leader. One of the hallmarks of more highly developed human beings (and bosses too, of course, they being humans and all) is their degree of in-the-moment self-awareness.

Let's look at just **three levels of awareness:**

1. Some managers are **not at all aware of their own behavior or its impact**. For example, a manager who is curt and cool with her staff when they don't get right down to the business at-hand. She shuts down even the briefest bit of rapport, such as asking "how has your day been going?" (and waiting for the answer). Not only that, she has no idea how this behavior distances her from her staff.

2. The manager **comes to realize that she does thi**s. She wants to change what, she realizes, is a deeply ingrained behavioral pattern that is not serving her well as a leader. So she adopts a new habit–doing a bit of a reflection after she has a meeting or shorter interaction with a staff member. She runs back over in her mind how she started the meeting and what the employee's reaction was. She draws some conclusions as to how well she did applying her more "connecting" approach and vows to do better next time.

3. The manager has **developed her awareness to where it occurs in the present, not after-the-fact**. Now, as her employees enter her office, she is conscious–in real time–of what she is saying to establish a personal connection and how they are responding to her approach. If she doesn't feel that enough rapport has been created, she extends the casual conversation a bit longer until it does feel right.

My example here was around the human acknowledgement and connecting that we, as a species, seem programmed to need before we interact. In fact, however, we can apply these three simple levels to any behavior we engage in.

The most effective leaders have mastered this competency. They know what they are doing, saying, thinking, feeling and responding as it is happening. They are exhibiting Emotional Intelligence.

# No Choice:
# You Have to Take Your Own Path

The late great expert on mythology, Joseph Campbell, used to tell a tale from the days of King Arthur. One day during a feast, the Holy Grail appears high in the great room but draped in a veil. Then it disappears. The bold Sir Gawain proposes that the knights all go off to find the cup and behold it unveiled. Just about all of the knights choose to follow existing paths through the forest, none of which lead anywhere near the grail. It turns out that to have even a chance of glimpsing the chalice, a knight has to divert from the well-worn path he is following and set out hacking through the deep, tangled brush, creating a brand new path.

It is like this in organizations. So many managers strive for great results and success (i.e. the Grail) by playing it safe (i.e. taking a comfortable path). They are careful to agree with their boss, not rock the boat, fit in, do things the (so-called) tried and true way other managers there do, be perfect so no one can catch them making a mistake, micromanage and drive their staff so they themselves will look good in the eyes of upper management, lash back when criticized instead of learning from the feedback, and so forth.

This is what The Leadership Circle (TLC) calls the *reactive* approach to leading. It smacks of dependency on what others think and what they might do to you if you don't do what they expect you to do.

Research by TLC reveals a lot about those managers who generate the best results, who (here comes the metaphor) find the Grail. They engage in creative leadership competencies around *relating*, being *system-savvy, self-aware* and *authentic*, and placing high priority on *achieving stretch goals*.

These best bosses have the courage and persistence to shift gradually from a reactive leadership style toward an outcome-creating one. This takes guts. It calls for faith in oneself. It requires the humility to learn from mistakes and face one's shadow side that is holding one back from greatness.

A lot like that Knight of the Round Table who decides to step off the path, raise his sword, and start carving his way into the dark, unknown depths of the forest.

# Did You Ever Try to Climb a Lattice?

For at least 40 years we have had the idea of "lattice" organization as an alternative design to the traditional hierarchy which assumes employees all want to climb up the ladder. In lattice organizations (and, beyond W.L. Gore & Associates, there weren't many of them out there back then), you could go in any direction—up, sideways, and even down—to keep your learning, development, and capacity growing.

Well, the lattice concept is back with a vengeance. Deloitte includes the *shift from ladder to lattice* as one of twelve trends featured in its 2011 Human Capital Trends report. Organizations today are flatter, with a much more diverse, gender-balanced workforce that is motivated by things like work-life balance, opportunities to work remotely, professional learning, work variety, collaborative, team-based work approaches... and not necessarily by promotions to the C suite.

This trend has implications for you, the manager. Here are a few that come to mind for me:

- A given employee may be, at different times, your direct report, peer, internal client, boss, and perhaps your employee again.
- You will be called upon to coach and develop not just job specific skills and knowledge but also general competencies that will transfer well to other roles and functions the employee may perform in his/her career journey across the corporate lattice.
- With more career options and employees who, collectively, are motivated by such a wide range of outcomes, be careful not to assume that you know what your employees want. Actually asking them becomes even more critical.
- And especially don't assume that your employees are all waiting patiently for you to quit, retire, or get transferred so they can move up into your position.
- You will be expected to develop your people for the greater good of the organization, not just for your own operation.

Talent development, especially in larger companies, is becoming more complex but it will make the work experience much richer, for everyone…including you, the manager.

# Coaching vs. Mentoring

Whatever your field and whether you are a manager or individual contributor, you can benefit greatly from feedback and advice as you navigate the currents and shoals of your career. As I look back over my own journey through the world of work, the times when my career was most stagnating was when I was into myself and not challenged by any input from anyone.

How about you? Do you have access in your life to a trusted advisor? When was the last time you challenged yourself to grow and become better? Or, if you are a leader, do you have an employee who is ready to expand his or her capacity? Is one of your direct reports stagnating, in coasting mode?

Maybe it's time for **a coach...or a mentor.** In case it is, here's my quick take on the differences:

- First of all, you can find both coaches and mentors internally, within your organization, or externally.
- Coaches...
  - » Usually have professional training in guiding, advising and challenging others.
  - » Engage in a contracted role in aid of specific goals and outcomes the client wants to achieve.
  - » Bring a process, a formal structure, which they customize based on the needs of their client.
  - » Work in a regular, reasonably intense pace over a relatively short period of time (generally, from a few weeks up to one year)
  - » May be asked to help the client address issues around inadequate job performance, specific skill development for current or future positions, or career development in general.
- Mentors...
- Typically are older individuals with broad career experience & accumulated wisdom.
- Possess a deep knowledge of the organization, its culture, history and politics.

- Engage in a less formal, less focused, process of periodic, conversations with their "mentee."
- Support and advise, may also advocate overtly or behind the scenes on behalf of their mentee.
- Serve in the role of a trusted advisor, someone to run ideas and challenges by for advice.
- Help more generally in the area of personal effectiveness and development.

While I do executive coaching, I think coaches and mentors can work hand-in-glove. I usually encourage my coaching clients, once our time together comes to an end, to seek out a mentor for ongoing, periodic advice, course corrections and an occasional timely boot in the backside.

Can your direct boss be a coach or a mentor? Yes, absolutely, as long as he or she has the skills and the genuine intention to help the employee grow.

# Employee Engagement

When you think of new buzzwords in the lexicon of management and organizational performance these days, you can't escape "employee engagement." And with good reason. There has been a lot of research coming out recently that shows how much more your "highly engaged" employees contribute to the enterprise than your moderately engaged or disengaged staff.

Just as is the case with employee motivation and job satisfaction, ultimately it is the employee who decides how engaged he or she is at any particular point in time.

The good news is that senior decision makers and mid level managers can have a huge impact on the level of employee engagement throughout their organization. But first you must be willing to treat engagement as a strategic factor that supports your capacity to achieve the immediate goals and longer term sustainability of the enterprise.

And before you decide to incorporate employee engagement in your strategic decision-making, it helps to understand what it is, what management can do to foster more of it, and it's impact on business results.

# Employee Engagement-Just Part of the Puzzle

I recently attended a "Leadership Briefing" presentation, organized by Leadership Fairfax, which featured two stimulating Towers Watson consultants, Max Caldwell and Jennifer Meder.

The latest TW research is revealing that to generate a climate where your employees contribute at a consistently a high level of their capacity, you need more that just "*engagement*." You must add into the mix *enablement* (a better term for what used to be called empowerment), and *employee well-being*. Here, very briefly, is what constitutes each element of what they call "the 3 E's":

> *Engagement* – employee commitment, both rational and emotional, to contributing discretionary (i.e. more than mere "satisfactory" performance requires) effort to their job.
>
> *Enablement* – provision of the tools and resources necessary for employees to be able to perform in their job. Along with items such as technology and budgets, this includes skill training, appropriate authority to decide and act, and access to necessary information, etc.
>
> *Employee Well-Being* – a state of emotional and physical wellness, along with the belief that senior management genuinely cares about them. Forces that reduce well-being include too high a level of stress and burnout, psychologically toxic work groups or supervision, and poor habits around exercise, nutrition, and getting enough sleep.

This makes more sense to me than just stopping at engagement. An employee who has the will to perform close to his or her potential still needs to be properly equipped and be in a well state to deliver that level of performance.

And the boss can have an impact on all three "E's."

# Two-Way Communication and Engaged Employees

Hewitt Associates' *2010 Best Employers in Canada* study has some useful messages for all companies. (http://was2.hewitt.com/bestemployers/canada/pdfs/Hewitt_BES2010_results_release_Eng.pdf)

They assessed three factors:
1. STAY – Willingness to remain with your current employer
2. SAY – How positively you talk to others about your employer
3. STRIVE – How motivated you are to go above and beyond to contribute to the business success

Among the 50 "Best Employers," the average employee engagement score (i.e. % of employees who responded positively to all three factors) was 80%.

Particularly important, I think, are two key Hewitt findings.

First, there was two-way communication. To quote the Hewitt news release:

> *"One characteristic common to all organizations with high engagement is open, transparent, complete and timely two-way communication. During the last year, employees were well aware of the challenges the organization was facing, understood the possible solutions, proactively offered input, and committed to the course of action the organization's leaders decided to follow."*

A second finding, employees in these high-engagement companies exhibited:
• Support for improving productivity
• Willingness to make trade-offs in benefits over the shorter term (e.g. reduced salaries and work hours to enable colleagues to be retained on the payroll)
• High trust and confidence in their leaders.

So, once again we see the impact of *excellent leaders* who foster *open communication* leading to *trust*. Especially in tough times, your people will demonstrate greater patience, resilience and discretionary effort when they trust you and your colleagues in management.

# Positive or Negative Feedback Trumps None at All

A recent issue of *Workforce Week* shares the results of a nuanced piece of data on performance feedback, from the Gallup organization. They surveyed 1000 US employees, placing them into three groups based on whether they felt their supervisor gave feedback focused on:
- their strengths
- their weaknesses
- neither (the latter group they called the "ignored").


Of the group that said their boss focused on **strengths**, 61% were "engaged" in their work. 45% of those reporting a boss who attended primarily to their **weaknesses** were engaged but, at the same time, 22% were "actively disengaged."

But here's the shocker. For employees whose boss essentially ignored both strong and weak points, in other words, gave no meaningful feedback at all, virtually none of these (2%) were engaged and the rest were either neutral or disengaged.

"But, wait a minute," you say, "maybe engaged employees, the keeners, are more inclined to see their boss as noticing and commenting on their strengths. Besides, since they are engaged, they probably are demonstrating their best talents on the job anyway. Their boss is just noticing what's clearly evident." This, of course, is the classic question with a correlation between two variables: which one is influencing which?

Let's not go there. Instead, just *consider the consequences of not giving your people any concrete feedback to speak of. It can severely dampen your employees' level of engagement in their work.* With all the data out there linking employee engagement to business results, we are talking lost productivity and creativity—big time!

25% of that "ignored" group of employees had a boss who gave no feedback. I hope you wouldn't have been one of them.

# It's Not Too Late to Attend to Your Talented Employees

Right Management, in a recent newsletter, *The Shrinking Talent Pool*, laid out four pieces of data that managers would do well to take note of:

1. (late 2009) 60% of employees planned to pursue new job opportunities as the economy improves in 2010.
2. 54% of companies report having lost top talent during the first half of 2010.
3. 54% of employees have been approached by outside organizations in the last 12 months to discuss job opportunities.
4. 80% of employees say their workloads have grown in the wake of layoffs, their trust has eroded, and they are feeling increasingly discontented.

Now, I know that these are just statistics. They don't necessarily suggest the situation where you work. But, then again, maybe they do…

If it has been a rough few years for your enterprise, you may have–not surprisingly–been distracted from giving those staff still with you the attention they need, especially in tough times. And when we talk about your top talent, the ones that will be difficult and expensive to replace, this is a critical consideration.

So, here is just a quick reminder. Especially with your key talent, have you been…

- Indicating and reminding them that they are valued?
- Talking with them about their ongoing learning and development, in current and potential future roles in your company?
- Listening closely to them and scanning for their concerns and how they are, in fact, coping?
- Monitoring their work, not to overload them?
- Keeping them aware of the organization's priorities and strategy and where they fit in?

These are ways you can have a positive impact on employee engagement levels and reduce the huge cost of turnover of your best people. And, if you look at the list, none of these cost very much…other than some of your time plus the energy required to sincerely attend to their well being.

# Leadership Makes a Difference–at Every Level

In the US Federal Government, as many studies have also shown for private industry, **leadership**–especially at the senior level–is the primary factor determining how employees view their workplace. This comes from the 2010 report on The Best Places to Work in the Federal Government.

The report distinguishes between leadership at the executive level and at all managerial levels.

**Senior Leadership** – the level of respect employees have for senior leaders, satisfaction with the amount of information provided by management, and perceptions about senior leaders' honesty, integrity and ability to motivate employees.

**Effective leadership from managers** – the extent to which employees believe leadership at all levels of the organization generates motivation and commitment, encourages integrity, and manages people fairly, while also promoting the professional development, creativity, and empowerment of employees.

In both the private and public sectors it is employees' perceptions of senior leadership–much more than how they see their immediate managers–that has the greatest influence on the degree of emotional and rational attachment staff feels for the organization. Emotional and rational attachment is also called "employee engagement."

Nevertheless, as the BPTW study reinforces for this slice of the public sector, the immediate boss has huge impact on the work and career satisfaction employees experience. Not only is she a conduit to the culture, priorities and values of the larger organization, she is in the best position to make tangible things happen for employees at the micro level of their own job.

For these reasons, organizations are wise to invest their development dollars at both levels of their management structure.

# Isn't "Employee Engagement" Just Another Way to Get Them to Work?

A rich debate blossomed overnight in a long string of comments to a recent blog post by CV Harquail where she lays out "three reasons why employee engagement is a scam."

Here reasons are:
1. It focuses on the individual only as an employee and not as a whole person.
2. It seeks to get more discretionary effort from staff without giving a lot back.
3. What the engaged employee contributes to his employer can't be taken with him when he leaves.

*If your employee chooses to give extra effort and creativity to her job, is she really getting the short straw in the relationship?* That depends on whether you think the following outcomes that highly engaged employees typically seek are a fair exchange for added contribution to the enterprise:
- challenging/interesting work
- more say in how your work gets done
- career development and learning opportunities
- a collegial work experience
- opportunity to make a difference
- opportunity to experience yourself frequently in a "flow" situation (aka "in the zone").

I happen to think these are worth a lot, thank you very much. If you adopt an internal strategy of getting more of your employees to move into the "fully engaged" column, you can do it only if you inquire about and attend to your employees' needs, especially the higher order needs contained in the above list. Engagement occurs when the employee is fairly compensated for his performance AND experiences some of these outcomes.

You still have to have the basics of performance rewards in place. It's when you try to engineer good feelings without paying for the work done that an employee engagement strategy becomes a scam.

# Five Engaging Questions around Employee Engagement

I had the good fortune to attend a half day session conducted by the research and consulting firm, BlessingWhite, called "Impacting Engagement in 2011: The Leader's Role," It was to roll out findings from their global study, Employee Engagement Report 2011.

I want to share **five reflective questions** (with the permission of BW) that I took from their materials. These are terrific ones that you can ask yourself, as a check-in about your own level of engagement, and then share your answers with your staff. They are also great, of course, to ask your employees, individually.

Here they are:
- When are you most engaged at work?
- Why did you join this organization?
- Why do you stay?
- When you consider the organization's future, what are you most excited about?
- What are you most anxious about?

When you think about it, these can trigger deeper discussions in many directions. They can elicit important information about the current state of mind and well-being of your staff. And, handled well by you, they can grow the level of trust between you and your reports.

I strongly recommend that you visit BlessingWhite's web site (http://www.blessingwhite.com) to see the solid research they offer in the areas of Employee Engagement and Leadership.

# Employee Engagement in Action–an Example

I actually came across this article from Forbes.com in 2009 but never got around to sharing it.

The piece tells about Douglas Conant, the new CEO of Campbell Soup Company, who came on board in 2001 and over the next eight years grew earnings per share by 5-10% every year.

His strategies included invigorating their work force by concentrating on employee engagement. In 2002 62% of employees reported being *not actively engaged* and 12% were *actively disengaged.* By 2009, 68% were *actively engaged* and only 3% remained *actively disengaged.*

I love Conant's line:

> *"To win in the marketplace, we believe you must first win in the workplace."*

Here are several things the company did to "win in the workplace":
- Declared a "Campbell Promise": Campbell valuing people, people valuing Campbell
- Replaced 300 of 350 leaders within three years, backfilling half of the vacancies from within
- Surveyed employees annually and reviewed unit results with the respective managers
- Established *ability to inspire trust* as the number one criterion for evaluating managers
- Celebrated accomplishments, including lots of notes and letters coming out of the CEO's office

Recent major studies reveal that most powerful driver of employee engagement is the perception within the ranks that senior leadership cares about the well being of staff.

# Time to Tune Your Radar in to Your Staff

During the tough economic times you've tried hard to keep as many of your people on the payroll as you could. Perhaps those who were retained felt a measure of gratitude for your heartfelt intention to preserve their jobs. Do they still feel these good feelings? It appears to depend on what you've been demanding from them since. And many organizations have been asking too much for too long.

A recent study published by the Employee Engagement Survey company, Modern Survey, (http://www.modernsurvey.com/news/?p=508) has detected a trend that merits any manager's attention. Since 2007 they have been tracking semi-annually five questions that they connect with levels of employee engagement, the percentage of employees who:

1. Takes pride in the company
2. Intends to stay with the company
3. Goes "above and beyond" (what's expected of them)
4. Recommends the company (as a place to work)
5. Sees a promising future at the company


In February 2010 the percentage who responded affirmatively to all five questions dropped from the previous survey, conducted in August of 2009. **The first two declines** are statistically significant:

1. (Takes Pride) from 79% to 73%
2. (Intends to Stay) from 63% to 57%


You can read a summary commentary from Modern Survey. Clearly, many staff members are approaching the burnout stage. This has depleted both their energy for their work and their positive feelings toward their employer. Here's my take on it and what I would advise my managerial clients to do.

**First of all**, if you have been distracted with the challenge of keeping your enterprise or institution solvent during the recession, it's time to shift some of your attention to the current state of your employees' state-of-mind and well-being. This is especially true for those stars and "solid citizens" whose loyalty and consistent performance enable you to sleep at night. Talk to them. How are they doing? How are they keeping up with the seemingly never-ending extra workload? How can you make things easier for them.

**Secondly**, as a consultant at Modern Survey recommends, express your appreciation for their hard work, positive spirit and performance contribution over these tough economic times.

**Finally,** (re)start investing some resources in their development. Send them to conferences and courses that keep them current in their functional/technical expertise. Put in place a leadership development initiative for your managers and supervisors. This does two things. It gives them an immediate benefit they may not receive elsewhere and it tells them that you mean it when you say they are valued partners in the success of the enterprise.

# Hey, Employers. Will Your People Be Staying with You?

There is mounting evidence that many full-time employees, especially the best ones, are not happy with the way they have been treated during this horrendous downturn. A recent article in *Workforce Management* (http://www.workforce.com/section/news/article/studies-fall-employees-discontent.php) reports on two recent studies that suggest you might want to review if you have been neglecting your people. It's entirely understandable if you have, what with all the pressures just to keep the revenues up and the ink flowing black.

Here are several findings from the research quoted:
- 60% of **employees** intend to leave their job as soon as the economy turns around.
- An additional 27% are actively networking with an updated resumé in hand.
- 90% of **executives** would take an executive recruiter's call
- more than 50% of them are currently looking for another employer


Regardless of how accurate these data are, they do remind owners and executives not to forget the people management aspect of running the firm day-to-day. You cannot afford to neglect how your people are faring, even though they have a job and perhaps don't appear terribly worried about losing it.

My colleague, Scott Campbell and I authored an article earlier in the 2009 maelstrom with seven actions you can take in your organization. You can read our full piece at "Down the Slope and Up Again: Seven Strategies to Lead Your Team through the Recession." (ww.888fulcrum. com/down-the-slope-and-up-again-seven-strategies-to-lead-your-team-through-the-recession/)

Here are the strategies we recommend:
- Pay attention to the messages you are sending.

- Make the tough decisions quickly but don't just react.
- Focus on the vision.
- Keep people informed.
- Involve people with today.
- Demonstrate caring – even when letting people go.
- Invest in your leaders and key players.

Your people want to be appreciated for their contribution (which, because of the times, is probably well beyond the norm). They want to know what your organization is doing to remain strong in order to survive and move forward. They worry that their learning and professional growth has been on hold for the last 12 months and are looking for reassurance that you will be investing in their skills again soon.

If you neglect your people or take them for granted, you run a huge risk—many will be joining that group of folks already looking over the fence watching for when the grass over there starts to get greener. I wonder how many of yours already are?

# General Management

Most of the blog posts I have selected for this book fit fairly logically into one of the nine sections above. There were a number of select additional posts, however, that I really wanted to include but they were more of the stand-alone variety.

Here they are, in no particular order. All of the topics they address I think are worth the time of a busy manager to consider.

In particular, let me draw your attention to two entries that reflect issues I hear all the time in my work with clients:

- For supervisors, *Who Am I, a Boss or a Friend?*
- For managers, *Delegation, the Forgotten Management Tool*

# Hire to Complement Your Strengths

I once worked for a fellow named Ray. He was an combative, dedicated HR manager who had come up through the ranks without a lot of "book larnin'." While he saw most issues in black and white terms and was rough around the edges, Ray was wise, street smart, and fair in his personnel-related decisions.

When he took in yours truly on a transfer from another branch of the company, I had been recently hired with a masters degree from Cornell. Here was I, with my soft, nuanced approach to everything and full of organizational and motivational models I was hankering to try out, working for a boss with a bulldog, no nonsense style.

One day over a coffee I asked him, "Ray, why did you end up selecting me? We are so completely different, like day and night. The way we come at this work is so different too." He looked at me with a grin and said, "That's exactly why, Ian." You with your fancy degree and theories help to balance my shoot-from-the-hip style."

Ray was a man comfortable in his shoes. He was not at all afraid to have an employee who was stronger in some areas than he was. He understood what many managers don't get: you can accomplish much more when (1) you are aware of the skills and knowledge you lack and (2) you consciously hire people who complement what you already have.

It has been over twenty-five years now and yet I have never forgotten that brief conversation with my boss. And, you know, he wasn't the only one who was rounded out by his decision to hire me. I am still drawing on all that I learned from observing Ray in action.

# Who Am I, Boss or Friend?

This is a huge issue, particularly at the supervisory level and especially when someone is pulled out of the work group and promoted to supervisor. It becomes confusing for all concerned, the new boss and the staff. How to act? What to expect from one another? Can we still be friends? How to set new boundaries? These questions reflect the confusion and uncertainty that typically ensues.

At the front line, people have less experience dealing with the subtleties of human relations in an organization. Not surprisingly, the promoted individual tries to keep it the same as before. Listen to our new supervisor:

> *"These employees have been my friends for ages. I've laughed, played, drunk, and shared personal problems with them. I know many of their families, personally. They are still my friends even though I'm their supervisor. I mean, none of us have changed. We're all still the human beings we were before I received this promotion, no?"*

No!

While, yes, he/she is the same person and so are they, the situation has changed and the relationship must too. In their new book, *Being the Boss: The 3 Imperatives for Becoming a Great Leader,* Linda Hill and Kent Lineback lay out four critical ways the boss/employee relationship differs from a purely friendship one:

- Friendship is an end in itself. At work, however, the end is accomplishing work. If getting the job done conflicts with the relationship, the work must come first.
- Friends are equals and treat one another as such, while the boss carries more authority (and status, for that matter).
- Friends accept each other unconditionally. Managers assess their staff and press them to get better in their job and improve their skills.

- Friends (at least the trusting ones) don't check up on each other. Bosses expect progress reports and follow up on work done by their staff.

If you find yourself tempted to reach out to your employees as friends, don't go there. It is a minefield and you will surely step on a mine, sooner rather than later. That said, do of course treat your staff as fellow human beings, deserving of respect, concern for their welfare, and support in their job and career success.

Just don't buddy up.

# People Just Want to be Noticed... and Appreciated

I came across a quote from Oprah Winfrey, interviewed in the Dec. 26/10 issue of *Parade Magazine* :

> *"Everybody just wants to be heard...Do your eyes light up when I enter the room? Did you hear me and did what I say mean anything to you? That's all they're looking for. That's what everybody is looking for."*

In a word, we all want to matter in some way in the eyes of those around us.

This is useful information for managers. It doesn't take a lot of time or effort to send out signals to your employees that they matter:

- Ask questions of them and genuinely listen to their answers. Then, ask a follow-up question.
- Discover (don't just feign) an interest in their work and their life beyond work, should they wish to share a bit about it.
- Check in with them periodically re how they are doing in their work and their overall state of well-being.
- Notice and acknowledge to them when they perform well in their job, excel in a task (e.g. make a great presentation in a meeting), or go the extra mile at work.

Finally, thank them not just for doing but for **being** as well. It sounds something like this: "I'm really glad you are part of this team, Tom. I enjoy working with you."

# The Other Way, Beyond Technology, to Leverage Your Investment in Your People

"Our people are the key to our success." How so very often we have heard executives mouth these words. But then, how very often we have also heard their people mutter words such as, "Oh yeah, well, if we really are the key, how come they don't… "

Of course, it is true. In this increasingly competitive, knowledge-based and customer-driven economy your people are absolutely vital to how your enterprise performs. After all, pretty well everything that is done in your organization is done between and through people. Yet, it never ceases to amaze me why management powers-that-be don't devote more effort to accessing all the talent that they have paid for. There is such a phenomenal additional return to be generated if they only would.

I am going to assume you are not like "them." I am assuming you do want to access some of that rich untapped potential contribution of your employees. How do you go about it? Well, you have essentially two ways.

The first is through what most companies the world over are rushing to do—leverage employee production through *technology*. It's no surprise that technology is the fulcrum of choice. It brings results relatively quickly and these results tend to be clear and measurable. You can calculate a rate of return on your investment in technology. And there is no question that high-tech processes and information management systems have had a remarkable impact on the speed and quality of analysis and decisions people make.

But while technology tools leverage our interfaces with machines,information and distance, there remains a second, much deeper reservoir of untapped employee potential. I refer to *the human element*—what some people call the "soft side." This element involves both an internal and external focus.

The most successful and effective individuals possess a strong internal will to do better, to contribute more, to stay focused on results, and to grow and become even more effective. They intrinsically value other people and work hard at mastering interpersonal skills and a better understanding of themselves. The impact of this emotional intelligence is superior effectiveness when dealing with such external situations as:

- interfaces with other people in and beyond the organization
- customer/client service
- resiliency in face of challenges and change
- bringing out the best in staff
- harnessing group synergy for creativity and fast results

The good news is these attitudes can be developed and these people skills can be learned. All you have to do is move the fulcrum…

In physics, you move a **fulcrum** along a lever to create mechanical advantage. This increased leverage enables you to apply the same amount of **force** and move a greater **weight**.

In your organization, the "force" is your investment in the salaries, wages, benefits, and allocated fixed costs of your people. Three key "fulcrums" are

- the leadership style of your managers and supervisors
- the processes and interpersonal dynamics of your teams, and
- the personal accountability which your individual contributors accept for their performance and their interpersonal effectiveness. The "weight" moved is the results your people ultimately generate.

You deserve a high leverage return on your investment in people… and it is there for the taking.

Let me suggest the learning curriculum your organization should be offering in order to access that part of your people's potential that shows up for work but does not get put into play. The recommended programs are grouped under the three key fulcrums mentioned above: Leadership, Team Synergy and Individual Contributor Effectiveness.

# Leadership

Nothing inspires people more than great leadership. At its core lies the persistent application of vision, involvement of followers and a belief in their fundamental ability to perform well.

Leadership is not just for top executives. Nurture it at all levels. Teach it to your managers, supervisors, project leaders and lead hands. Whether guiding a department through a period of transition, creating a supportive, gratifying atmosphere for staff, or coaching the best out of a struggling performer or high potential employee, the aspiring leader must be sensitive. He or she must be aware of both the impact of his/her own style and the current needs, fears and hopes of those whom he/she leads. Your leaders should be learning how to:

- Manage through others
  - » Motivating and focusing staff
  - » Recognizing and rewarding results achieved
  - » Developing an optimum style
  - » Clarifying vision, mission, values, and priorities
  - » Ensuring high performance standards and results
- Coach for individual and team performance
- Manage change and personal transition
- Deal with conflict, resistance and so-called "difficult people"
- Run a meeting effectively

> *High performing teams focus on results*
> *and are willing to address, when required,*
> *how they are working together.*

# Team Synergy

A "team" can be a group of functional managers, a distinct department, a self-directed work group, or a temporary project team. Whenever people collaborate to perform a task or make a decision, we have a potential minefield of conflicting perceptions, agendas, needs and work styles. High performing teams focus on results and are willing to address, when

required, how they are working together. Teach your teams how to:
- Boost their performance by…
  - » Understanding human dynamics in groups
  - » Establishing agreed-upon operating guidelines
  - » Clarifying deliverables, expectations, roles and leadership
  - » Creating trust and openness
  - » When stuck, taking time out to deal with it
  - » Building individual member buy-in to a shared vision
- Tap into the creative potential of the group
- Kickstart a newly formed team
- Deal with conflict, resistance and so-called "difficult people"
- Run a meeting effectively

## Individual Contributor Effectiveness

Individual effectiveness combines a distinct set of skills with a clearly defined attitude about one's personal accountability in life and work. The skills, which all can be learned, fall into four essential categories:
- **Self-Direction**—Establishing purpose and goals for your job and career
  - » Identifying (and updating) what is important to you
  - » Determining your personal strategic career direction
  - » Planning, to transform your job and career goals into action
- **Self-Awareness**—Of one's own style, needs, preferences and impact on others
  - » Taking stock of your skills, knowledge, experience, attitudes, external resources and overall current situation
  - » Obtaining feedback on how your style is experienced by others
- **Self-Management**—Daily focus on priorities and maintenance of positive mental, emotional and physical states
  - » Self-organization & time management
  - » Harnessing cognitive and creative capacities through mental techniques
  - » Performing well during pressure and stress
  - » Maintaining health and physical fitness

- **Self-Presentation**—Expressing yourself in a variety of ways
  - » Clear, assertive face-to-face communications
  - » Networking and influencing others
  - » Projecting the appropriate, professional image
  - » Concise and persuasive writing
  - » Negotiating for win/win

While you cannot pay your people to want to put out extra effort, your leaders can help coax it out and your teams can foster a spirit of going the extra mile. But, ultimately, it is up to the individual. What is your organization doing to develop these skills and attitudes? Focus on them. Move the fulcrums. Leverage your people investment for organizational and business success.

# It's the Same Stuff, Even at Google

Google, I'm sure you will agree, is a business built on metrics and analytics. Well, they recently completed an comprehensive, rigorous internal study about what made great managers...at Google. The New York Times article says that Google wanted to *build better bosses*. Now, that certainly strikes a positive chord for me and boy does it sound familiar too... :-)

After all the sexy compilations and machinations of the data, the company came up with eight elements. They called them the **"Eight Habits of Highly Effective Google Managers"**: (parentheses below contain my own comments)

1. Be a good coach (frequent meetings, involving balanced, useful feedback)
2. Empower your team (vs. micromanaging them)
3. Show interest in employees' success and well-being (ah, that would be genuine interest, by the way)
4. Be productive and results-oriented (i.e. the soft skills approach coexists with hard results)
5. Be a good communicator and listen to your team (the flow goes both ways–frequently and authentically)
6. Help employees with their career development (do you see a connection with #3?)
7. Have a clear vision and strategy for the the team (this one makes every list)
8. Have key technical skills, enough to advise the team (i.e. you don't have to be a geek yourself)

What strikes me is that in such a technical environment the technical skills component of a good leader is not a heavy one. It barely makes the list, at number 8.

Scanning the list, I pick up a theme of **connection and involvement with staff**, without being terribly directive, except around vision and strategy. This confirms **the importance of a manager's role as a coach**.

We simply must hold our managers accountable for their ongoing coaching relationship with their employees. This means,

- giving these activities sufficient weight and rewards in the organization's performance management process
- teaching your managers how to coach
- freeing up enough time from other immediate demands on their attention to allow them to exercise the coaching role

Heck, if it's good enough for Google...

# A Great Read for Implementing Change

So much has been written about change, much of it fluff, some of it good. An eternal truth for leaders who would institute change, however, is that **you must understand and be sensitive to *people*.**

By people I mean (1) individuals who will be required to make changes in their own ways of working and being and (2) sub groups (units, departments, functional experts, age cohorts, etc.) that share certain views, values, and history.

Do you have to deal with a complex change in your organization or are you advising someone who does? If so, here is a book that speaks to you.

*The Practice of Adaptive Leadership* is written by a trio of respected and seasoned experts in the field of leadership. Pooling their individual consulting experience, they have laid out their collective take on the subject. They offer practical ideas and wise insights to help you make the calculated interventions you need to make in order to bring about the change you seek.

I wrote a book review (http://www.888fulcrum.com/the-practice-of-adaptive-leadership/) on it but let me share just a few highlights here:

First, distinguish between *technical* challenges and *adaptive* challenges your organization faces.

- **Technical challenges** – problems that can be pretty clearly defined and addressed with known solutions using the help of technical experts.
- **Adaptive challenges** – these forces require significant (and often painful) shifts in people's habits, status, role, identity, way of thinking, etc.

Many leaders immediately see a challenge as a technical one that requires a course of action calling for technical expertise (hey, what a coincidence!) that they possess. The book leans against this tendency by focusing on how to identify and then respond to adaptive challenges which, by their nature, are more complex and less clearly defined and resolved.

Second, you must keep shifting your position between being "on the dance floor" where you are are actually taking action, making interventions, trying things out and "in the balcony" where (looking down on the "dance floor") you strategize, observe patterns, form hypotheses and think through options about how best to proceed.

Finally, I love how the authors keep coming back to the leader himself/herself whose own fears, perceptions, and comfort levels have such a huge influence on the ultimate success of any response to an adaptive challenge. It is extremely tempting for a change leader to blame other people or forces when the transition process bogs down. The wise leader periodically asks herself, "How am I contributing to the situation?"

The book comes with lots of practical, "how-to" tips and approaches. Check it out.

# Ensuring HR Has a Seat at the Table

At a recent HR networking event I attended Alice Waagen, President of Workforce Learning LLC, presented on "The Top 5 Skills for Human Resource Professionals." One of her five struck me as by far the most critical for HR's success in any organization: **"Business Acumen."** Interestingly, this was the one that generated the most lively discussion among the attendees.

Under "business acumen," Alice included a basic understanding of the classic elements of business: finance, marketing, strategic planning, production, customer service, and the role of technology. By the way, this applies for any sector—private, public, or not-for-profit.

Why is having this broad knowledge important? Because HR professionals need to understand the world of the line side of the enterprise if they are going to be a *trusted advisor* to their internal client(s). Yes, trusted advisor. This is the other and more critical role of HR, beyond ensuring compliance to corporate human resources related policies and processes.

But in order for HR to achieve genuine trusted advisor status, let me suggest two additional skills under *Business Acumen*:

1. **An understanding of the specific "business" of the organization.** What are the key products, services, production processes, strategic plans, challenges, infrastructure strengths and weaknesses, and so forth? This gives them "street cred" with managers on the line side. In addition, it enables HR folks to provide informed input, especially at the C-level, on key business issues that arise.

2. **A good sense of how successful sales people build and maintain relationships.** Good sales people (and trusted advisors, by the way) develop a deep awareness of their client's concerns, fears, hopes, desires, assumptions, biases, etc. Similarly, HR folks should be able to look at problems through the filter of their client, while adding value by applying their professional human resources prism to the mix.

For example, the VP of Field Operations is concerned that customer service attitudes are poor and causing retail sales to drop. HR makes an evidence-based case that the culprit is weak management skills leading to low front line staff morale. How to proceed? The savvy HR manager frames the goal in terms of getting sales back up. This is what he talks about when proposing any training initiative or other intervention to boost morale. Fix the sales problem and you've earned the respect of the VP. *How* you do it is not high on your client's list of concerns.

So, if you are in HR, make sure that you understand your organization's core business. Then position your role as, first and foremost, supporting the enterprise's success. And, if you are a non-HR executive, insist that members of your Human Resources department learn what they need to know about the business of the business in order to earn that seat at the table of decision-makers.

# The Checklist is Not the Goal

Reading Jack Zenger and Joe Folkman's brand new book, *The Inspiring Leader*, I ran across an interesting quote:

> *"Many people believe that they will be judged by what they don't accomplish rather than by what they do accomplish."*

In the spirit of full disclosure, I have a deep—and almost always unfulfilled—need to complete every task I assign for the day. So, I write this as much for me as for my readers.

Effective individuals get a lot done AND what they get done are the most important accomplishments on their plate. This is what it means to be *effective*. It is true that, looking back, we bask in the glow of our most valuable, meaningful, and challenging accomplishments. We don't dwell on the fact that last June 5 we didn't get around to doing task #7 on our "to do" list. Nor do we spend much time regretting that our lower priorities for the year never were achieved.

**Perfectionism is not our friend!** It drains precious time away from the highest leverage tasks. Also, it causes us to fritter away precious energy by obsessing on getting one task just right before moving on.

**Now, as a manager,** be aware of when your people dwell on doing a better job on a task than is necessary and when they migrate to completing lower priority tasks to the detriment of what's most critical. Let them know what you regard as most important. Also notice when they are doing a lower priority task just because at some point they had committed to doing it.

In closing, a note to self. My purpose is to best serve my clients and manifest my vision for me and for my firm. Completing every item on today's task list is not the measure of a successful day. But, boy, it feels so good when I do! Therein lies the rub.

# Delegation: The Forgotten Management Tool

*"I never get to the truly managerial parts of my own job."*

*"I'm staying too late at night and working too many weekends."*

*"_____is really ready to advance but I have no job to promote him/her to right now."*

*"If I don't give my best people some new challenges soon, I may lose them."*

Sound familiar? Is this what you find yourself saying (or thinking) these days? You've tried all the time management techniques. You've even upgraded your software and tried (unsuccessfully) to re-negotiate your job objectives with your boss. And you have some talented people that are demotivated by doing the same duties month-after-month.

Maybe it's time to consider delegating an element or two of your job.

## Why We Don't Like to Delegate

But wait a minute! We managers are not natural delegators. We're pro-grammed to exercise our authority. We got to this exalted level in the organization by successfully solving problems, not passing them off to others.

There are at least six reasons why we resist delegating a task or deci-sion to our staff. Here they are below, along with our "self-talk" that accompanies them:

### Power

If I hold on to the task or at least retain the final say over it, I maintain control. They must continue to rely on me. No, thank you. I'll do it myself and stay the "boss."

**Trust**

I just don't trust them to do the job properly (i.e. to my satisfaction and standards). They're not ready yet, anyway. They lack the experience. Besides, if they blow the job or make a bad decision, it could be costly…and you-know-who will have to answer for that. No, it's safer to do it myself.

**Self-Confidence**

If I hand off a basic duty or decision like this one, what will I do? Truth be told, I'm not sure how to do some of those higher level, strategic type tasks in my "manager" job description. No, it's easier for me to look busy and on-the-ball by doing lower-level tasks that I know I can handle.

**Fear**

My staff is already overloaded and they don't hesitate to remind me of the fact. If I approach them with something new to do, they'll be really angry. I can just hear them now, "Oh yeah, and just which part of my job do you expect me to drop in order to do this extra work for you?" No, it's just less confrontational to do it myself.

**Time**

I will take too long to show them how to do this. Besides, I can have it done in the time it takes just to explain it to them. And this way I won't have to spend time coaching and checking up on them. No, it's less hassle to do it myself.

**Feels Good!**

Man, I love that sense of accomplishment when I complete a task, make a decision and solve a problem. I can check it off. I can tell others about it. Why would I want to give up this great feeling? No, I'll hang on to the task, thank you very much.

## How to delegate

*First of all, select what to delegate.* Pick a task or new responsibility that is perhaps less challenging to you but will stretch and develop the employee(s) in question. Then, stipulate the goal-the result you are looking for-and how it will be measured. But take a caution from no less a leader than General George Patton: "Never tell people how to do things. Tell them what to do and they will surprise you with their ingenuity."

*Secondly, decide on how much authority you will give them.* Clarify which decisions they (1) can make totally on their own, (2) can make but keep you informed, (3) must run by you first for approval, (4) will be making jointly with you, or (5) must have you make for them. The best practice is to hand off as much as you personally can tolerate and the situation will allow.

*Next, clearly communicate precisely what you are delegating.* Cover what is to be done, by when, why (the background and reasons), allowable resources, any limits on their authority for decision-making and, of course, the benefits to them for taking on this responsibility. As you strive for mutual understanding and agreement, allow them to push back, to negotiate around the parameters…this is what independent people who take on full accountability for their commitments typically do before they make a commitment that they intend to keep!

*Then, check for mutual understanding around what was agreed.* Sometimes employees are reluctant to disagree directly with you. They may not agree or understand but they say "yes" to you anyway because they don't want to come across as dumb or difficult.

*Provide support, as appropriate.* This may mean just being available if they need you or you might go so far as to schedule periodic progress update meetings. Nevertheless, this is your opportunity to coach, guide, challenge and encourage your protégé. employee(s).

Finally, follow up, evaluate and recognize work well done.

Recent research from the Gallup organization indicates that the most prominent practice of "great managers" is finding the right fit between employees' skills and the work to be done. Delegating is a great way to create that "right fit."

Too many managers overlook the power of delegation as a development tool. Former CEO of AES, Dennis Bakke, had his "80/20 rule." It said that AES people should spend 80% of their time on their primary roles (i.e. their job description duties) and 20% on special tasks, giving advice, learning new skills, and projects not necessarily related to their official job. This ensured what work was challenging, motivating and, yes even fun.

What can you delegate and to whom? Why not create some opportunities? Even if you don't do it for staff development, do it to free yourself up for that part of your job that really justifies the big bucks they pay you.

# The Paradox of Who Makes the Decisions

Leadership Coach and blogger, John Agno, laid out eighteen lessons on leadership from Colin Powell. (http://www.coachingtip.com/2010/02/leadership-lessons.html) One particularly caught my attention with its application to the non-military organizational environment:

The day soldiers stop bringing you their problems is the day you have stopped leading them. They have either lost confidence that you can help them or concluded that you do not care. Either case is a failure of leadership.

As John mentions, sometimes leaders foster a culture that asking your boss for help is a sign of weakness or failure. This can have really negative consequences for the organization because employees will not tap into the experience and wisdom of their boss when it is appropriate. In the end they risk making poor decisions that can cost a lot.

But the real issue here involves, as is so often the case with the art of management, a paradox:

**On the one hand** you want your people to take full account-ability for their job, including making decisions and taking action without always running to you to solve their problems or provide cover by endorsing decisions they are about to make.

**On the other hand**, you want your staff to come to you when they are truly stymied, the cost of a bad decision is too high, or they need information that is understandably beyond their reach.

The "art" here is, when an employee brings a problem to your doorstep, to be able to differentiate between a problem that they should be able to handle on their own and one on which it is appropriate to consult with you.

Make a point of clarifying with each of your direct employees what sorts of issues or situations should trigger their talking with you first.

You can do this as part of a larger conversation about the performance expected from them. Part of their performance, after all, is bringing their independent judgment to bear in their job. These guidelines, of course, may need to be adjusted as you go forward, so be sure to revisit them periodically, as needed.

Finally, having done such a good job clarifying decision boundaries, resist the ever-present temptation to break these guidelines by taking the "monkey" and solving a problem that clearly belongs to them.

# About the Author

## Ian Cook, MILR, CSP

It was in a class at McGill University called "Personnel." (yes, that would be Human Resources today) when Ian first became drawn to making a lifelong professional contribution to management development and leadership.

The professor was talking about the universal tension in organizations between the needs of the enterprise and those of its employees. In an instant Ian knew that wherever his career took him, he would be involved in finding ways to reconcile these seeming incompatible demands.

He began his career in Air Canada, first in airport operations and then in a variety of roles within Human Resources. He later moved to become the very first Organization Development manager at Honeywell Canada. There he worked on projects around the development and alignment of talent within the company. It was in 1988 that he decided to launch out in his own enterprise by founding, along with his wife Linda, the leadership development firm, Fulcrum Associates Inc.

Ian is a professional speaker, trainer, facilitator and executive coach. His expertise and passion lies in what he calls "micro leadership," helping the mid-to-executive level manager lead effectively in that interpersonal space between himself/herself and the individual employee. As he often says,

*"Effective micro leadership practices yield macro results!"*

Ian received a Bachelor of Commerce from McGill and from Cornell a Master of Industrial and Labor Relations degree with an emphasis in Human Resources Management. In addition he has been a lecturer at Ryerson University's Faculty of Business.

He has a Diploma in Gestalt Theory and Methodology from the Gestalt Institute of Toronto. This has helped immensely to hone his effectiveness as both a group facilitator and an executive coach.

Ian is a Certified Speaking Professional. CSP is the highest earned designation conferred by National Speakers Association, The Canadian Association of Professional Speakers, and the Global Speakers Federation.

Ian gives back through his volunteer involvement with the community leadership organization, Leadership Fairfax Inc. A 2004 alumnus of the LFI program, he has served on the Board of Directors, chaired their Program Committee, and currently presents to the current class of LFI's Emerging Leaders program.

# About Fulcrum Associates Inc.

Fulcrum Associates Inc. was founded in 1988 as a leadership development company offering training workshops, keynote presentations, executive coaching, and facilitation services that help managers get consistently high performance and greater results from their employees.

Fulcrum's over 200 clients from the USA and Canada include some of the largest corporations in the private sector, major trade and professional associations, small business, government, and not-for-profit organizations.

They know Fulcrum for programs that present thought provoking approaches and practical techniques to help managers:

*Create a motivating work environment
and foster commitment in their employees
to deliver superior results.*

The company works with its clients to customize learning & development solutions that achieve the particular results they require. Three areas of particular expertise are:

1. **Micro leadership** (for macro results) – An appropriate blend of classroom workshops and post program support strategies addressing the skills that are essential for managers to foster an engaged and productive team of employees.

2. **Evaluate to Win**™ – A strategic business management system that aligns the efforts of all employees with the mission, values and priorities of the organization. Jack Welch calls Evaluate to Win "the best business management system I've ever seen."

3. **Top team development** – Highly customized team coaching strategies, supported by the assessment tools of The Leadership Circle®, whereby executive teams foster a leadership culture that maximizes the performance contribution of employees across the organization.

Find out more about Ian Cook and his work at

www.888Fulcrum.com

Feel free to contact Ian at:

888-385-2786 or ian@888fulcrum.com

# Finally, A Strategic Employee Evaluation Tool, created by business people for business people!

*"Evaluate To Win is the best Business Management System I've ever seen."*

– Jack Welch

With **Evaluate to Win** (ETW) you create Alignment throughout your employee population and cascade Performance Requirements from the very top to every corner of your organization. It is a tool designed to foster and maintain a culture of WINNING.

ETW's navigation and dashboards enable senior leadership to drill down and see, at a glance, how a particular organizational level, a department, a team, or even a specific individual is performing.

Your managers and supervisors will have regular, meaningful conversations with their employees around how well their behaviors align with the Mission and Core Values and what performance will support the Strategy and help the enterprise be more successful.

To request a personal overview of ETW, please contact:

**Ian Cook**

888-385-2786
ian@888fulcrum.com

Fulcrum Associates Inc.
1711 Pine Valley Drive
Vienna, VA 22182
USA